Alexander Robert Charle Dallas

The story of the Irish church missions

an account of the providential preparation which led to the establishment of the

Society for Irish Church Missions to the Roman Catholics in 1849. Part 1

Alexander Robert Charle Dallas

The story of the Irish church missions
an account of the providential preparation which led to the establishment of the Society for Irish Church Missions to the Roman Catholics in 1849. Part 1

ISBN/EAN: 9783744736114

Printed in Europe, USA, Canada, Australia, Japan

Cover: Foto ©Lupo / pixelio.de

More available books at **www.hansebooks.com**

THE STORY

OF THE

IRISH CHURCH MISSIONS.

PART I.

AN ACCOUNT OF THE PROVIDENTIAL PREPARATION
WHICH LED TO THE ESTABLISHMENT OF THE
SOCIETY FOR IRISH CHURCH MISSIONS
TO THE ROMAN CATHOLICS
IN 1849.

BY THE REV. ALEX. DALLAS, M.A.,

RECTOR OF WONSTON, HANTS,
AND HONORARY SECRETARY TO THE SOCIETY.

"The very hairs of your head are all numbered."—MATT. x. 30.
"Behold, there ariseth a little cloud out of the sea, like a man's hand. . . . . And there was a great rain."—1 KINGS xviii. 44, 45.

LONDON:

PUBLISHED FOR

The Society for Irish Church Missions,
11, BUCKINGHAM STREET, ADELPHI;
AND SOLD BY
MESSRS. HATCHARD AND CO., PICCADILLY; NISBET AND CO.,
BERNERS STREET; SEELEY AND CO., FLEET STREET;
AND MACINTOSH, PATERNOSTER ROW.

HARRILD, PRINTER LONDON.

PREFACE.

IN giving a history of the Society for Irish Church Missions to the Roman Catholics, in order that a correct impression should be conveyed, it was absolutely necessary to explain in detail the very first links in the chain of events which led to its formation. This will account for the authorship having devolved on me, as none other was intimately acquainted with the minute circumstances of the preparatory steps. This also will serve as an apology for the personal character of the narrative.

The Chapters have been published periodically in the "Banner of the Truth;" but it has been felt that the interval between the publications breaks the current of interest in the whole. The account of what may be considered the Providential preparation for the organized development of the movement occupies fifteen chapters, twelve of which are found in the pages of the "Banner." They are now published together, as the first part of the history of the Society.

The events recorded in this Volume are sufficient to prove that the preparation in the minds of the Roman Catholics of Ireland for receiving Scriptural instruction existed before the famine of 1847. That calamitous event did not produce the desire to receive the teaching of truth from Protestant sources, though it tended to remove many prejudices, and so to increase the feeling which already existed. The records in these pages will also show, that in spite of the prejudices and fanaticism of some, the Roman Catholics of Ireland can be approached with the teaching of the true gospel in distinct antagonism to the religious notions in which they have been nurtured, without provoking that measure of violence and danger which some have feared. Honesty of purpose kindly shown, combined with patient endurance of opposition in good temper, will ensure such a hearing as gives encouraging hope of some success, which, by the blessing of God, is always realized. This is abundantly proved in the following narrative; and when the second part shall appear, detailing the operations of the Society which was formed in consequence of these events, an immense amount of additional proof will be shown.

It is greatly to be regretted that, with all this evidence, the means for carrying on the work placed at the disposal of the Committee should be so inadequate to the requirements of the case. Of all the attempts made to pacify Ireland and benefit the Irish people, none have been crowned with such success as have the efforts of the Irish Church Missions; and if ten times the amount at present employed were contributed by Protestant Christians for this work, the results already obtained justify the expectation that the blessing of God would accompany the offering, and Ireland would become characteristically Christian and Protestant.

November, 1867.

CONTENTS.

	PAGE
CHAPTER I.—INTRODUCTORY	1
CHAPTER II.	6
CHAPTER III.	15
CHAPTER IV.	24
CHAPTER V.	35
CHAPTER VI.	45
CHAPTER VII.	60
CHAPTER VIII.	74
CHAPTER IX.	87
CHAPTER X.	102
CHAPTER XI.	121
CHAPTER XII.	137
CHAPTER XIII.	151
CHAPTER XIV.	166
CHAPTER XV.	176

APPENDIX.

		PAGE
I.—A Voice from Heaven to Ireland	....	197
II.—A Look out of Ireland into Germany	....	203
III.—Irishmen's Rights	....	215
IV.—The Food of Man	....	223
V.—Constitution of the Society	....	228

THE Story of the Irish Church Missions
TO THE ROMAN CATHOLICS.

CHAPTER I.

INTRODUCTORY.

IRELAND is said to be England's difficulty. In a political point of view this has become a proverb. There is another phase of the matter, in which men's souls are considered before their social condition. In this aspect "danger" might be substituted for "difficulty" in the proverb; and the words "chastisement" and "remembrancer" might be added to awaken in the mind a sense of the "danger." Ireland is England's chastisement. England has made an unrestful bed for herself, and she must lie upon it. If she is scourged, she furnished the rod herself. In the twelfth century Romish England planted Popery in Ireland. The upas tree was an exotic unknown in the country; the soil was prepared by treachery; and the instrument of the actual transplanting was the sword. Upon the coincidence, solitary in all history, when an English pope could conspire with an English king, this baneful act was accomplished, and so Ireland became popish. When, in the sixteenth century the dark cloud of Romanism was rolled off the shores of England, by that "wind" that "bloweth where it listeth," no prayerful pains were taken to carry on its course over the sister island; to "say to the wind, Come from the four winds, O breath, and breathe upon these slain, that they may live." Laws were made to anglicise the Irish, instead of efforts to Christianize them. The royal supremacy of the King of England was established, and not the supremacy of the Majesty on high. The means employed consisted of Acts of Parliament, and not the Book of God. These sins of England have been fruitful in constantly-recurring chastisement—fruits that are full of danger to the sinful nation. "Be sure your sin will find you out."

Ireland is England's remembrancer. How is it that the British power has become what it is? A vast variety of means have concurred, during a long series of years, providentially combining to constitute an empire unparalleled in history, overpassing the old Roman world. It seems as though a morsel of earth had been broken off from the rest of the world, and floated out into the ocean as a special spot on which to plant that which is as the tree of life, the leaves of which are for the present the healing of the nations—the Holy Scriptures. Secured by insular position, it pleased God by His grace, to nurture the growth of this precious plant in Britain, and then to extend the empire to reach the ends of the earth, so that British influence finds its way into the midst of all nations. Surely its mission is to scatter the seeds of the life-giving truth in its worldwide path, and to convey this bread-fruit wherever it carries its merchandize. Is Britain fulfilling its mission? Alas! no. And God has ordered that a sort of practising-field, having the most pressing call for scriptural influence, should be placed within a stone's cast of the privileged garden of this tree of life; a community, itself a part of England's empire, so bound to Britain that both must feel together in weal and in woe. On this practising-ground England's mission of mercy should be seen, plainly and powerfully carried out. For many a long year, England's high duty, the condition of her greatness, has been nationally neglected everywhere—in Ireland as in India; but Ireland lies as it were in her bosom, to be a thorn in her side, painfully reminding her of this neglected duty—a difficulty—a danger—a chastisement—a remembrancer, that if she did but rise to her duty and take care that, with the wise acts of Parliament, the people should have the wiser word of God—for "the foolishness of God is wiser than men"—Ireland would be a help instead of a hindrance to England.

That which the nation at large will not acknowledge to be a duty, and which does not enter into the national policy, the faithful few, the little flock, those who recognize God's hand in the rise and fall of nations, attempt to effect by the combination of their weak efforts, trusting to the blessing and power of Him with whom "it is nothing to conquer, whether with many or with them that have no power." God has condescended to accept such efforts, and to honour them by employing them for the accomplishment of results which nothing but Divine power could effect with such an instrumentality. Ireland has been the scene of these marvels of disproportion between the means and the results; and it would appear to be for the glory of God that the course of events by which His Providence worked with His grace in the process should be laid open before the Church of Christ. One who has been honoured by being permitted to work in the matter from an early date, has been urged to write the story. On long and full consideration it seems plain, that the most marked interventions of the finger of God are to be observed in many of the minuter events that formed the history: and these can only be fairly detailed in a personal narrative, from which there has hitherto been a shrinking. But advancing age deadens the sensitiveness which shrinks from personal revelations. Time is rapidly passing; the story must be told now, or may never be needed; and therefore, with the blessing of God, the Story of the Irish Church Missions shall be made public, although it involves the necessity for a personal narrative.

CHAPTER II.

In order that a just judgment may be formed of any movement amongst a people, there must be some knowledge of their previous condition. This alone can prepare the mind to understand the necessity for the movement, and the exciting causes which produced it; or to judge rightly of the means by which it has been originated and carried on. This preparation is especially required for Englishmen with respect to Ireland. It is not too much to say that there is more correct knowledge of our distant dependencies than of Ireland diffused amongst the people of England. Almost every Englishman acquires, somehow or other, a notion of an Irishman, in which the prominent features are caricatured, and the redeeming qualities are merged; and this incorrect image has to be erased from the mind before a true photograph can be impressed there. A careful examination into the Story of the Irish Church Missions would much assist in the process of such an alteration in the minds of Englishmen; but to do this there should be the preparation of an adequate knowledge of the former state of things in Ireland. What seems to be wanting is a reply to these three questions— 1. Was there a necessity for the work of the Irish Church Missions? 2. Has there been a suitability in the instrumentality? 3. How was the instrumentality produced and applied?

After much consideration, it appears to be the best course to take these questions in the reverse order, and show—1. How the instrumentality was produced and applied. This will go some way towards enabling the reader to judge of—2. Its suitability; and will bring out very distinctly—3. The necessity for the work of the Irish Church Missions. It is the conviction that this course will be the simplest and the shortest way of conveying a correct view of the missionary movement towards the Roman Catholics in Ireland, that has required the adoption of a personal narrative, as the best mode of telling the Story of the Irish Church Missions. To that personal narrative I now ask the attention of the reader.

Men measure results by the means which produced them. These may be considered as inadequate, but still some kind of relative proportion is sought for to justify the result. It is not so with God. He veils the appearance of directly miraculous interference by the employment of some instrumentality, but He magnifies his own power and retains his own honour by making use of the most insignificant means in accomplishing vast results. "The very hairs of your head are all numbered"—numbered for use by the Divine hand. The metaphor is supplied, not by the muscles and powerful limbs of our body, but the weakest fibre that it bears. This precious word unfolds the history of many a marvellous work through weak agency.

I gathered in my early years those English notions of Ireland to which I have already alluded. A familiar friend of my father was an officer who had served in the rebellion in 1798, and as a boy I drank in from him all the horrors of Vinegar Hill, and Scullabogue, and Wexford Bridge. I never for a moment thought of going to Ireland. In the early years of my ministry I actively and earnestly advocated the cause of the Church Missionary Society, and especially the promoting of

Christianity amongst the Jews. I often went on deputation for these Societies. In the year 1840 I was at Bath for the Jews' Society. My colleague in this deputation was the Rev. Anthony Thomas, who was the secretary of the Irish branch of that Society. The meeting at Bath was a very interesting one, enlivened by a little discussion, in which I took part. Mr. Thomas was attracted by this, and pressed me to undertake to represent the Society at the annual meeting in Dublin, which was to take place in a few days. I peremptorily refused. We were nearly a week together in Bath, and Mr. Thomas pursued me with an untiring persistency which more than wearied me, and did not win me. I never had a wavering feeling on the point. I left Bath, and travelled on the outside of the coach of those days, which was full of passengers. Only one place remained vacant, as we sat only three behind the coachman. We changed horses at Melksham, and were already in motion, when a porter stopped us with the bag of a gentleman, who soon followed him and occupied the vacant seat next to me. This was Mr. Thomas. I remember his first words, " This is surely providential." He continued his appeals to me during the journey to Marlborough, a single stage, the only distance he had to travel, and as he left the coach there he extorted my consent.

I relate these particulars because they form the centre point of a cluster of lines that have opened to a vast extent in the circumference, which includes the Story of the Irish Church Missions. I don't remember ever to have had a more settled determination than that which produced my refusal at Bath, and I was surprised at myself when I had allowed Mr. Thomas to carry away my consent at Marlborough. There were no electric telegraphs in those days, or I might have at once retracted my promise; but it was ordered in Providence that I should go; and I have often felt thankful that these "numbered hairs" satisfy myself, that it was not my own will but God's will that took me to Ireland.

In the ensuing April I arrived in Dublin in the week of the meetings. The Tuesday in that week is the day on which the anniversary of the Jews' Society is held. After a speech which conveyed many statistics, interesting when read but which failed to keep alive the interest of an Irish audience, my turn came to speak; and, profiting by what I observed in the previous half hour, I called my hearers into the region of prophecy, and drew a picture of the Jewish prospects, when "the remnant according to the election of grace," shall have been converted, and the effusion of the Spirit shall descend upon "all Israel." My speech was received with enthusiasm by the people and acceptance by the platform, where I found that I wanted no further introduction to be received into brotherly intercourse by the warm-hearted clergymen that filled it.

At the clerical meetings which occupy the mornings of the "April week" in Dublin, I met upwards of two hundred of the clergy (the number has since reached five hundred). These meetings were very striking, and altogether new to me. I was called on to speak, and received an attentive hearing. In fact, I seemed to have been carried on the top of the wave far over the shore, into the heart of Ireland. I have no false modesty in saying this, because it was too rapid a feeling to be excited by an estimate of merit, for which there was no time; and because I feel it to have been a part of the preparation, designed in Providence for the work God purposed to do afterwards.

While this providential preparation was thus made in the kindly feelings of Irish clergymen and friends, it was completed by the revolution which was produced in my feelings about Irishmen and Ireland. I was brought to Dublin at a time when there was a gathering of what may be called the cream of a large class of the clergy, and I gained in a week the experience of Irish heart that could hardly have been obtained in a year's detail of intercourse all over the country. I had a bird's-eye view of Ireland with the sun shining on it, having passed through the lower clouds of prejudice as in a balloon. I saw how much there is to be valued—how many compensating features in favour mingled with those that may be unfavourable in the Irish character. In short, I found myself suddenly placed in an entirely new position, with new affections called forth, awakening a lively interest in a people amongst whom I found a warmth of kindness readily responding to my new feelings.

For four or five years I cultivated this friendly feeling by frequent intercourse. I gladly undertook the deputation of the two Societies I have named, from time to time, into many of the principal towns and districts of Ireland. I attended the April meetings regularly; and while I received a general kindness from almost all whom I met, I contracted intimate friendship with many of the excellent Christian men who adorned the Irish branch of the United Church. Amongst those who have passed into the presence of our Lord I may mention especially Denis Browne, Dean of Emly; Horace Newman, Dean of Cork; Arthur Wynne, Arthur Guinness, and others, whose praise is in all the churches. In the early days of my intercourse with the Irish clergy these were as nursing fathers and brothers to me.

It was not until the year 1843 that my attention was especially drawn to the state of the Roman Catholic population. It seemed as though the previous years were required to enable me to take root, as it were, in the character of Ireland, before I was called to the task of acting upon it for the glory of God in the conversion of Romanists. I had had much experience of Romanism in continental countries, and had carried on a kind of mission amongst Romanists when I resided in France. This was one part of the necessary preparation for the work of Irish Church Missions. It was necessary that a knowledge of Irish character should be combined with this; and having now obtained such a knowledge, my mind and heart were aroused to observe the condition of the Romanists of the country to which my affections were newly drawn. Here began the events which gave birth to the Society for Irish Church Missions, and with this I will begin the next chapter.

CHAPTER III.

It has often been a matter of surprise in the retrospect that I should have been interested in Ireland for so long a period without having my attention drawn to the condition of the Roman Catholics. Having for many years mingled with the Romanists, and seen practical Romanism by the candle-light of the world, and afterwards looked upon it in the broad sunlight of the Gospel, it would have been natural that Rome in Ireland would have been the prominent point that struck me in the prospect. When I carried on a little mission to Romanists in France, I had been painfully sent to school to learn Roman doctrines and difficulties by an early discomfiture of my untaught zeal in earnest controversy with a priest of high talent. Yet, during all the time included in the second chapter, the case of the Romanists had hardly crossed my mind. One of the addresses I delivered to the assembled clergy in Dublin was published as a tract, under the title of "Realizing, the strength of an effectual Ministry." It would seem strange that the application of such a subject on such an occasion in that place could have been made without reference to the most real of the difficulties of an Irish ministry of the Gospel. Yet the address did not touch on the point. I trace in this unnatural restraint another token of the purpose of God as developed in the work He has given me to do. It was needful that the affection for Ireland to be planted in my heart, and the kindness towards me to be planted in the hearts of Irishmen, should take root with sufficient grasp to bear the shock of the storm to be raised by the course of controversial aggression which was the object in the dealings of Providence. An earlier observation of the real state of things would have led to an earlier entry on that course; and the position and the acceptance of the innovator would not have ripened so far as to fit him for the work.

The first dawn which I can recall to mind of an awakened sense of the condition of the Romanists in Ireland, is connected with an incident of encouragement in the ministry which I will relate.

There are usually meetings of clergy in Cork after the Dublin April meetings. One year I attended these, and remained during the following week to deliver a course of lectures on the Second Advent, in the church of my excellent friend the Rev. T. Finny. Within a fortnight I delivered twenty-one different addresses in Cork; and being completely exhausted after the last Sunday's work, I escaped from a host of friends, and retired incognito to refresh my spirit as well as my body amidst the mountains and the waters of lovely Killarney. I was quite alone, and allowed my thoughts to float away from all the subjects which had occupied them. I had no books, and should hardly have used them if they had been at hand; but in wandering amidst the charmed spots of beauty that abound there, a number of living books constantly crossed my path, and I could not but read on each human page the black story of deceit and death written there by Rome. Free from the excitement of any direct object for present active duty, these living epistles of error suggested a crowd of thoughts which were like clouds in the sky of my mind, obscuring the sunshine of the rest I was enjoying, and taking all sorts of shapes as they passed slowly across it.

The week passed, and Sunday came. I went to church, and fearing to break my quiet seclusion by meeting some who might know me, I took a seat by the door. The sermon pained me. It was a great mistake from the text, "If you would enter into life, keep the commandments." I longed to get into the pulpit and rectify the mistake. I had gone into the church hoping that nobody would recognize me, I left it breathing an earnest wish that somebody would meet me that could place me in the pulpit for the second service. Outside the door I found a gentleman and his daughter, who accosted me, guessing who I was—friends in Cork had bid them expect me to preach at Killarney. They said that several persons had come with that expectation. By a little management, I was introduced and permitted to preach in the evening. I laid open the Lord's way of enabling a sinner "to enter into life," and offered the only means of salvation through faith in Christ Jesus.

On the following morning I left Killarney. There were no railways then. I got on the outside of the coach on a fine May morning. As it was an early start, I had not had time for my morning's reading, and took out my Bible. A respectable woman was sitting next to me. At our first stop she said, "That's a good book you have, sir." "The best book," I replied. "I think, sir, you are the minister who preached last evening at Killarney church." "I am." And this led to a long conversation. She was a Protestant, and evidently one who felt the value of saving truth. She was a widow, and had a daughter married to a tradesman in Killarney—nominally a Protestant. They had entirely neglected religion, and by the force of circumstances around them, they were being drawn into Romanism. The mother had been very unhappy about her daughter, and had taken the journey from Dublin on purpose to strive to divert them from their intention. She had urged, and prayed, and struggled for a fortnight, all apparently to no purpose. She had entreated them to go with her to church before she left. They had refused in the morning, but softening under the feeling of parting from the mother, and saying openly that once going to church would not be any consequence, they consented to go in the evening.

"Sir," said the poor widow, "I took their consent for what it was worth—just a kindness to me, and thought much as they did, that it was little I could hope for from that, as respects the changing of their purpose. But I prayed, sir, with my soul's heart for the poor creatures, that God would stop them from being Roman Catholics, and save their souls. When the prayers were over, a strange gentleman began to preach. It was the gospel—the very truth of Christ—sir. I could have cried out in the church, but I was silent, only my heart was praying all the while. My Mary, sir, was crying, but she hid it. We got home, and from that very moment—supper-time and all—we talked, and talked, and they would not leave off and go to bed till past one o'clock, and then only because I was starting so early in the morning. And, sir, praised be God, they said they never had heard what they heard in that sermon; and, sir, they say they won't go to Mass."

I have related this as nearly as possible in her own words, which were deeply impressed on my memory, and I have related the incident because it gave the first perceptible impulse to that earnest spirit of inquiry into the condition of the mind of the Roman Catholics which brought out the strong conviction of their readiness to receive gospel teaching. And such an incident will be enough to excuse the omission of much detail in explaining how the conviction grew, for which there would be no time or space in this Story of the Irish Church Missions.

In looking back on the broad and deep stream of thought which soon after overflowed my whole mind for a time, I cannot discover its source in any perceptible beginning earlier than this. To trace it further I must look up to heaven. I ruminated on the Killarney incident all the journey home. The next time I visited Ireland, my keenest observation was directed to the Romanists. I have already said that I had acquired much experience in dealing with them in foreign countries, and I brought many practical remembrances to bear upon my new study in Ireland. I never shall forget a scene in Normandy. I was talking about Christ to a cottage full of peasants, and opening the gospel from the Scriptures, when a man cried out, " Have the goodness to read the second commandment out of the Bible." This had no special connection with what I was then teaching, but I turned at once to the twentieth chapter of Exodus, and read aloud, " Vous ne vous ferez point d'image taillée," etc. The effect was electrical. The people had listened before, but now they were moved. " Could that be the word of God ?" " Was it a real Bible?" "Impossible that the priests could know that to be God's commandment." "The Church was full of graven images, and everybody was taught to bow down to them." From that time there was life in my little congregation. Opposition and warm words from some, anxious inquiries from others. In a few months a little living church was gathered from the neighbourhood, a portion of Christ's little flock who continued steadfast in the faith. It led to an earnest controversy with the priest, and I was sent for by the *sous-préfet* to be dissuaded from "this folly," as he called it. But the work of the Lord prospered, and souls were brought out of darkness into the light of truth.

Thus I had learned a practical lesson which I applied in my intercourse with Irish Romanists. While speaking of religion, I put some such test as that which had electrified my French Romish congregation—Did they know the second commandment as God Himself had spoken it—"Thou shalt not make to thyself any graven image," nor "bow down to it"? Some pointed question, strongly and sharply making Scripture doctrine expose Romish dogma. This plan brought out character in a striking manner. It gave me frequent opportunities of perceiving the strange mixture of anxious desire for knowledge with the proud notion of possessing it—of rebellious doubt of the priests with cowardly crouching under their power.

It would be impossible to give any defined account of the steps by which my thoughts were consolidated into a conviction, that there was a preparation on the minds of many Romanists in Ireland to give attention to the teaching of truth, if only efforts were made by Christian men to meet Rome upon the ground of her errors, while at the same time the gospel of Christ was exhibited in its truth. This led me to consider what steps I ought to take, in order that advantage might be taken of the state of mind I perceived to exist, and that the means I proposed might be brought into operation. My intimacy with so many eminent and excellent men amongst the clergy led me of course to take counsel with them on this important matter. This shall be the subject of the next chapter.

CHAPTER IV.

THE last paragraph of the preceding chapter gave the result of the observations made in the course of many months. I promised that the present chapter should refer to my intercourse with many eminent and excellent clergymen on taking counsel with them on the subject of those observations. The sketch of this intercourse must condense the conversations which were spread over the same period, carried on from time to time, the details of which might swell into a volume.

Never shall I forget the surprise and disappointment I felt when I found, that those from whom I expected approbation and encouragement in the course I proposed, met my suggestions with disapprobation and rejection. They gilded this pill with much praise for zeal and godly earnestness, etc. This glittering outside scarcely covered the bitter "but" which was meant for medicine, while it turned all my strongholds into castles in the air. Each of my kind clerical friends had two very decided reasons why my observations could not tend to any good results. First, I was entirely ignorant of the Irish character, and could not therefore estimate the effect which my notions would produce if they were acted upon. How could I, as an Englishman so lately acquainted with Ireland, suppose that I could form a judgment in such matters? Then, secondly, the peculiar fervour of the Irish nature, inflamed by a tyrannical priesthood, would be sure to excite to bloodshed if any direct and open efforts to expose the errors of Romanism were attempted. In vain I pleaded my long and varied experience of human nature in Roman Catholic countries—the effects I had seen produced amongst excitable people under similar circumstances—the influence of honest openness in subduing prejudice—the historical evidence of the progress of Christ's religion everywhere from the beginning, and especially at the Reformation in England—the duty of Christian ministers placed amongst a darkened population—and the promises of God's Word applicable to the case. I did not then gain a single convert to my opinions amongst the valued clerical friends whom I consulted, every one of whom, I sincerely believe, was a Christian man, having the glory of God and the good of souls the great object of his life.

While I state these facts, I feel bound to give also the grounds which they had for their conclusions. My disappointment led me to inquire diligently and to study carefully the course of events which could have produced what seemed to me so strange a state of mind in such men as I have described. I am the more desirous of doing this as the knowledge I thus attained will be very useful to enable the reader to judge of the real condition of things in which the Irish Church Missions was to be born, and to struggle for life until it acquired its mature position. The inquiry was, I believe, a part of the necessary preparation for the subsequent work; and therefore that I was thus driven to it was one of the required steps—a link in the chain which God's Providence was forming.

There was a traditional feeling about the violence of Romish opposition, handed down amongst Protestants from the times of the Reformation, when such grievous mistakes were made by the government of Queen Elizabeth; and when the wily efforts of Loyola's first agents entwined into one cord the political and the religious feelings of Irishmen, making Saxon and Protestant, tyranny and heresy, convertible terms in their vocabulary. This naturally led to strong antagonism on the part of Protestants, and a similar combination of the terms rebel and Romanist, indicating a feeling which reproduced itself, and rendered the alienation more decided, engendering mutual hatred and terror of each other. The memorials of the massacres towards the close of the seventeenth century, and the recollections of rebellion at the end of the eighteenth, greatly fostered the fear of violence in the Protestants of the beginning of the nineteenth century. This was kept alive by the occasional outbursts of priestly power influencing the rabble upon electioneering contests, of which some egregious cases, such as that at Carlow, were prominently recorded. The tithe-war (as it has been called), which followed a few years after the Emancipation Act of 1829, and resulted in the concession by the government of a quarter of the tithe property, imbued the mind of the clergy generally with the idea, that the violence then manifested was specially directed against their profession; in this they mistook the object of attack, and confounded their religious character with the possession of the temporalities attached to their position. With these traditional feelings, fostered by these experimental notions, it can hardly be matter of surprise, that the altar anathemas drawn forth from prominent priests upon instances of aggression should be considered as tokens of systematic exercise of power, rather than the audacious threatenings of the bully.

While I suggest this to account for the timidity of many good Christian men, it is not to be supposed that there were not constant efforts made to bring the light of the truth to bear upon Roman darkness. Men whose praise is in all the churches of Ireland were not wanting, who showed a concern for the spiritual deadness of their Roman Catholic neighbours. Peter Roe in the south, Charles Seymour in the west, and Old Gideon Ouseley everywhere, stand at the head of a long list of worthies who laboured diligently for the glory of Christ amongst Romanists as well as Protestants. There are few clergymen who cannot testify that they have taken the occasions of funerals to preach the gospel at a grave, at which whole clans and factions have come to pay respect to the remains of some one of the old blood, Protestant though he may have been, while that respect has kept them silent and uncovered.

There have been besides, from time to time, seasons of temporary revival in various localities. Perhaps the most considerable was that which took place in the county of Cavan, about the year 1826, when large numbers of Romanists appeared to be impressed under the gospel teaching. Ancient prophecies were supposed to be dragged from the obscurity of old wives' traditions, to indicate that Romanism was to be banished from Ireland about that time; and superstition was thus called in to aid the work of the preacher and the Scripture-Reader. I believe that this, and every other awakening in which the salvation of Jesus is brought before the people, has left some tokens that his precious gospel has gathered some souls; but as a permanent influence upon any number of persons or locality, this revival has died away, and left no other trace than the few members of the little flock to whom I have referred.

As my inquiries led me to discover these natural causes for the state of mind in which I found my clerical advisers, I could not but observe that the great work I felt to be the duty of the day was only the more necessary from all I learned, and that none of these causes had any reference whatever to the course I proposed. The great error of the Elizabethan government was the postponing of all vital religion to the alteration of the supremacy from the Papal to the Royal. The hatred was built upon the political portion of the argument, and has stood upon that foundation ever since. The chief outbursts of violence under priestly excitement have turned upon elections or politics in some shape or other. The tithe-war was kindled and carried on for property and politics, and as a step in the great struggle in which emancipation was gained. The Christian efforts of individual ministers, and the teaching during periods of revival, have all been the simple declaration of the gospel as such, without any special reference to the false teaching of Rome placed in contrast. This gospel, where put forth with earnestness and simplicity, will never be without some effect, for "the word shall not return void;" but to deal with Romanists as such it is absolutely necessary to disabuse their minds of the false notions of Christian truth which they possess, and to show Christ's salvation contrasted with that which is not Christ's, though they are taught to believe that it is. The one thought laid upon my heart was, that a time was come when this contrasted truth might be put before Irish Roman Catholics plainly, simply, and openly, and that they would receive it. All my inquiries led me to see that this had never been done since the days of Usher and Bedell in anything like a suitable degree and manner; and all my inquiries therefore only settled me the more in the opinion which my clerical friends were so anxious to remove from my mind.

Many honest Irish hearts will revolt from my statement, that "this had never been done," because they will turn at once to the Irish Society, which holds a high place in Irish affection. I value that Society greatly; I think it was raised up of God to do a great work, specially suitable to the time when it began, but its object and operations did not take it out of the category in which I have placed the other efforts to carry the gospel to the Roman Catholics. The good men who commenced it in 1818 were true servants of God, and for their work they deserve the thanks of Irish Christians. The thought was a happy one. The Irish language has a great charm for the Celtic population. It is to them clothed with romance, and ornamented with superstitous attractions. Its character is difficult to read, and comparatively few can do so while most of them desire the attainment. The plan of the Irish Society is to employ persons who *can* read the Irish language to teach those who *cannot*. A small remuneration is given for each pupil, and the condition imposed is that the lesson-book should be the Bible. This is an admirable device so far as it goes, but it does not go so far as even to approach the point which I strongly felt to be the special requirement of the time—the open exhibition of the gospel of salvation placed in such a light as that its beams should be cast directly upon the errors of Rome openly exposed. I believed that this was the one thing wanted for Ireland; and I believed that the state of the people's minds would render such an exhibition of the gospel not only safe but successful.

The clergy whom I consulted were deeply attached to the Irish Society, and I think that, though unconsciously, the strength of their objections to my proposal was derived in great measure from the secret feeling that it might take the place of their favourite scheme. There need not have been any ground for this, as I had imagined that the organization already working so well would be the best means of effecting my object; and I suggested that the Irish Society should take up a new branch of operations, expanding and enlarging its work to meet the existing state of things. To this, however, objections were strongly urged. These objections were more strongly developed in the subsequent progress of events, and I will reserve any mention of them for their place in connection with those events.

I did not sit down satisfied under my disappointment. The idea had taken root in my heart, and it *would* grow. I talked to but few about it after what I heard from the clergy. But I did speak to one kind, clear-headed, and large-hearted friend, the late Arthur Guinness. When dining with him one day in a house he then had in Rutland Square, we were conversing after dinner, and when I asked him whom he thought likely to give me further information on the state of the people, he said, " Nobody could help you better than Fanny Bellingham." " Where is she ?" " Not a hundred yards off." " Will you introduce me ?" " Go and tell her I sent you." It was a summer's evening; I rose from the table and walked to Dorset Street at once.

" The hairs of your head are all numbered." This was the hair on which depended great events. My acquaintance with Fanny Bellingham opened an entire change in the course of this story, and its beginning requires a new chapter.

CHAPTER V.

That precious word, "the hairs of your head are all numbered," is the text of the Story of the Irish Church Missions. What a slender hair was that which led me from Rutland Square to Dorset Street? A walk of three minutes brought me into a room there, in which I found two ladies, probably the only persons in all Ireland who could afford me the help that I needed. Miss Bellingham and her sister received me with Irish frankness and Christian kindness. My pen shrinks from giving the name publicity, but it is historical now; the angels that ministered to her in her much usefulness in this work have finished their office, and borne the spirits of both into the presence of their Lord. The publicity that might be indelicate before is dutiful now —a duty to her and to her Lord, who worked by her instrumentality.

Some conversation soon brought out the sympathies on the subject that had been laid on both our hearts, and a few occasions of intercourse bound us together as fellow-workers. Fanny Bellingham intensely felt the love of Ireland which characterizes the people, but Divine grace had given a higher intensity to her love of Christ, and the two affections fused into one powerful impulse to save Irish souls. She was not faultless, but her very faults tended to further this impulse. Her mind had a colouring of romance, which might have marred her influence; but there was a compensating power of good sense which mellowed the tint, and left only the exciting interest of heightened expectation to her thoughts and her plans. She had for years been closely connected with the principal efforts for spiritual good to the Irish, and therefore possessed a fund of knowledge which through her friendship was at once transferred to me on all needful points. By this means I was better enabled both to estimate the difficulties of my adventure, and to distinguish the course to be pursued. It is essential to the right understanding of the Story of the Irish Church Missions that some of these difficulties should be laid before the reader, and especially as he will thereby perceive some important features in the state of the Irish mind at the time our first efforts were made.

There can scarcely be said ever to have been a time without some local attempts made by individual Christians to evangelize the Roman Catholics in Ireland. None of these however amounted to an enlarged systematic organization of general application until the year 1818, when the Irish Society was formed. In the preceding chapter I have explained the system on which the operations of that Society were arranged and conducted, and have expressed my sense of their fitness for the time and circumstances in which they commenced. There were some very attractive features in the plan. The necessary secrecy of the instruction—the novel mode of gathering the pupils—the picturesque descriptions of the schools on bogs, behind turf stacks and walls, etc.—the exciting danger of discovery by the priest—and above all, the interest in finding a Romanist teaching Romanists to read the truths of the gospel; all these gave a charm to the plan which commended it to Irish Christians, so that the Irish Society was embraced by them as the National Institution which was to evangelize Ireland.

There were, however, some serious evils underlying this pleasant plan, which were not duly estimated by the good men who formed the Society. The Irish mind is suspicious, as well as acute. It is ever ready to draw inferences according to its own tendencies. Irish Romanists have been brought up in the belief that the Roman creed is the only truth, that the Protestant profession is a modern and untrue religion, and that Protestants generally are well aware of these points. They suppose in charity that honest Protestants are ashamed of their position, and maintain it only for their temporal supremacy in Ireland. To counteract such views, a bold, above-board course was called for. Any other would be calculated to foster the feeling in which they had been educated. It would not produce that confidence in our faith which calls for respect, while it provokes discussion. It has been found that a misapprehension of motive had been produced on the minds of many who were connected with the Irish Society. But again, the necessary secrecy of the operations, to be carried on by a class of men in whom the inbred principles of Romanism dim the perception of the strictness of truth, opened a large door for deception, which the most vigilant exercise of caution could scarcely detect and counteract. Many painful instances testify the facility and extent to which such deception has been carried on.

But besides these, a still greater evil was essentially connected with the system of what was called the "mechanical teaching" of the Irish Society. The habitual estrangement between Romanists and Protestants in Ireland left the Irish clergy generally unacquainted with Romish habits of thought. Experience has shown that the dogma of Rome that the Church interprets Scripture rightly, and that none have a right to question on any point, effectually shuts up the mind against scriptural *thoughts* while reading the Bible. As an additional security, Rome has so arranged her teaching, that certain essential and important words suggest ideas to the Romish mind entirely different from the correct and literal meaning. In consequence of this, Romanists may read the Bible without gathering the meaning which the words are intended to convey; and it is only by the direct act of God's mercy, contrary to the ordinary course of things, that a Roman Catholic has power to receive saving truth from the words which, when rightly understood, "are able to save the soul."

Yet by that Divine mercy a considerable effect was produced in the first years of the new effort. Four years afterwards (in 1822) a similar society was formed in London, under the name of the London Irish Society. These two societies worked harmoniously, and many Romanists were engaged as "Irish Teachers" in several parts of Ireland. They reported the instruction of a number of pupils, and several were by God's grace induced to neglect the Mass, and brought much persecution upon themselves. The result of this was a demand for further instruction wherever there had been any real effect produced. The Irish Society system was as the thin edge of the wedge, and where it made its way it needed to be driven home. It was as the alphabet to the child, its use being to prepare for further knowledge. Progress would be the surest token of success. In some places there were evident marks of such success; but the good men did not seem duly to appreciate this evidence; they liked their system well, and determined to "let well alone." Applications for further means of instruction were not attended to, but discouraged.

Weak instruments are always most fitting to manifest God's strength. A Christian lady, with the spring of an Irish heart, determined to do something, though it were but little, to meet the demand for more instruction. The fathers of the Irish Society were so attached to their child as it was that they did not wish any alteration. They did not encourage this lady, and if she had not been closely allied to the most eminent of those good men, even *her* persistency might have been overcome. She was, however, allowed (but privately, and without printing her appeals) to ask for subscriptions to support a few Scripture-Readers, who were to be placed entirely under the control of the directors of the Society, though these private funds were to be quite separate from those of the Society. By this means three or four Scripture-Readers were engaged by this energetic lady, who gathered a few like-minded ladies to help on her work, and they formed what was called the "Ladies' Auxiliary to the Irish Society." The number of Readers gradually increased to ten or twelve, who were paid £15, £18, and £20 a year, collected by unceasing private letters written by this one indefatigable woman, who still lives, and still, at an advanced age, occupies her every hour in asking for supplies to support her little band of pioneers. It was a good many years before her work was publicly recognized, and still longer before any help was accorded to it from any Society's funds. The concession of such help became a turning-point in the progress of missionary work in Ireland, the account of which will occur in a future stage of this Story.

The partial efforts of these few agents produced more opposition and persecution than had been experienced before. Thrilling incidents occurred in consequence, and these formed a favourite topic with the public advocates of the Irish Society.

These Readers were a step in advance in the right direction; but the progress was discouraged, and it needed such buoyant and Quixotic spirits as those of Alicia and Fanny to keep their course under such circumstances. The general result produced no movement amongst the Romanists. Few were brought out of Rome, and very many continued the reading of the Irish Scriptures, and were passed as pupils again and again, who were as constant to the Mass as ever, and never thought of any change of faith.

It was not without great effort in urging a

further step in advance that I gave up the attempt. The difficulties through which "the Ladies' Auxiliary" lingered on its feeble life were warning enough; and though I earnestly pressed some of the influential men of the Irish Society in Dublin, their reception of my arguments made me relinquish in despair all hope of enlarging their machinery into missionary operations. I reluctantly ceased to communicate on the subject with my clerical friends in Ireland, and confined my inquiries to my correspondence with Miss Bellingham. At this time my health failed, and I was doomed by medical direction to ten months of inaction and travel for rest and change. The thought of the ripeness of Irish Romanists for Christian instruction never changed, and would not rest during this period. The absence of ordinary duties left the whole field of my mind open for the wandering thoughts which this one idea suggested. Plan after plan presented itself before me. Difficulty after difficulty arose, was combated, and gained the victory. At length some of these phantoms that used to "come like shadows, and so depart," left more permanent impressions on my mind, and were shaped into something that seemed feasible to a sanguine temperament.

The conviction that the object was for the glory of God and the saving of souls, together with the constant exercise of earnest prayer, rectified the excesses of this temperament, and made that appear possible which might seem scarcely so to the more phlegmatic. One plan at last took a shape. I can say now that it was of God, because immense difficulties have been overcome, wonderful results followed, and the evidence of Providential interference has been marked and certain. The development of this plan shall be given in the next chapter.

CHAPTER VI.

It seems to be a rule in the ordinary dealings of God with his people, that when his Spirit directs the mind to any work for his glory, his Providence will sooner or later concur in effecting the object. If a matter is laid upon the heart, the sure test that it is of God will be that openings will occur to render it possible. The trial of patience may be long; but the greater the delay, the stronger will be the proof that God's Spirit is placing the matter on the heart. To give up the desire is to prove that it never was of God. To maintain it in patience and diligence is to secure the accomplishment; and God, in his own good time, proves its origin by granting providential openings to ripen it to success.

Though in a long life I have had many evidences of this general rule, I never knew any like the instance of that feeling which, after long delay and great discouragement, has borne the fruit of the Irish Church Missions. The conferences with Fanny Bellingham in April, 1845, were occupied in transforming the abundant materials for discouragement into the occasion for discovering some means which might overleap them all, and work the spiritual enlightenment of the Roman Catholics of Ireland. Our schemes were very interesting; but every one had some impassable barrier, which rose between our intentions and the approach to the objects of our solicitude. I came to England without having imagined anything practical or possible; and Fanny and her friend left Dublin for a tour in the south and west of Ireland.

I happened to take up a paper which contained a statistical account of the wonders which had been achieved by the penny post—then not very long in operation—the facilities it afforded, the effects it might yet produce, etc., etc. It struck me that this might supply the means of reaching Roman Catholics over the heads, as it were, of the priests. It was a crude thought, but it was the seed of many mature ones. The great object which called for present action was to find some way of stirring the minds of a large number of Roman

Catholics, in such a manner as would test the truth of my conviction that there was a greater readiness to listen to Protestant teaching than formerly; and do this so manifestly as would lead the good men in Ireland to believe what I stated, and to come forth to take advantage of the favourable opportunity. The impediment to the attaining this object was the jealous watchfulness of the priests to hinder every kind of communication between their people and those who would bring them the light. Then, also, the difficulty of obtaining any machinery which could exercise an influence sufficiently extensive to produce the desired result was overwhelming.

But the penny-post took letters without asking the leave of the priest; and it was world-wide in its application. If only the names and addresses of every Romanist in all Ireland could be obtained, a ray of light from God's Word—an appeal to common sense and conscience might be made, which must create a movement amongst them. How to carry such a plan into execution? Immense difficulties were in the way; but I have often found it good to act upon the wise saying of the poet —"The wise and active conquer difficulties by daring to attempt them." So I pondered on this thought, and drew it out in various ways, and by degrees it took a shape that seemed less impossible, nay, feasible. Fanny had pointed out the failing features in many of my plans, which had been rejected. I wrote to her about this one; and before sending my letter, I prayed earnestly that we might be guided in coming to a decision in the matter. Her answer approved the plan warmly, and made valuable suggestions; so I settled myself into a determination to take all possible steps to develop this thought into action.

I was one evening musing or dozing in my arm-chair, in a dreamy way. A young friend was in the room, to whom I said, "Take up your pen, and write as I dictate." There flowed forth from me, literally without check or correction, that appeal to Irishmen which is entitled, "A Voice from Heaven to Ireland." As I read it afterwards, I was struck with the Irish composition, and I earnestly prayed God to own it as his own, by making it instrumental in saving Irish souls. It is too long to give here, but it shall be given in an appendix.

I was greatly encouraged by the fact that I had something to send to the Roman Catholics. It seemed to me a token that other difficulties would be overcome. But as I began to look at these difficulties closely and separately, they seemed scarcely surmountable. How to get the names of the people! How to get the means of sending a sufficient number of these letters by the post! How to get the whole organized and arranged without such publicity as would defeat the effect of the appeal! All these were very serious impediments to anything like a confident expectation of success.

While such thoughts as these were revolving in my mind, I one day received a letter from a gentleman, with whom I had been acquainted some time before, but I had not had any recent intercourse with him. It was but a little while since I had recovered from an illness; and a small tract which I had subsequently published had fallen into his hands. His letter spoke of my illness, and of his conclusion from the tract that I was restored to health; and he reminded me that, some time before, I had said to him that I would willingly co-operate with him in doing something for Ireland. Would I act upon that promise now?

The promise that he spoke of had faded

from my memory, but I felt that it was God's providence which had recalled it to his at that peculiar juncture. The letter came to me upon the very day on which I had mapped out a plan, which, of course, I had made complete in all its parts. The arranging into order of a multitude of desultory thoughts, it formed a very beautiful building to my imagination; but in my walk after breakfast I felt with a sigh that it was but a castle in the air, as it wanted the solid foundation of means to carry it into practice. The letters came; there were a good many; amongst them a small one in a hand which I did not recollect. I left it till the last, little knowing that it was to prove the means of obtaining the solid foundation which would turn my castle in the air into an accomplished fact.

In the course of my cogitations, I had ventured to put forth something of my penny-post plan to several Christian friends. I found that, without a single exception, they all looked upon the whole matter as an absurdity. If cold water by pailfuls could have chilled my hopeful expectations, they would have been frozen to death over and over again: but they were sufficiently alive when I received this letter to send me forth to visit my friend in

London, and to lay my imaginations before him. He did not seize upon the thought at once, but he did not reject it. He took time to make all I had said the subject of prayer and of consideration; and, in the course of several conversations, he gradually adopted my views, and agreed to undertake the expenses of certain arrangements. These opened the way for others more costly still, and God opened his heart to supply what was needed for expense, with a beautiful mixture of large liberality and careful wisdom.

It has pleased God to remove from this present life the friend of whom I speak, and it is a gratification to me to give my testimony to the disinterested earnestness with which he devoted his substance, his time, and his prayers to the great object of communicating Christ's gospel to the Irish Romanists. Mr. Durant, of High Canons, was a man of singular devotion to the cause he took in hand. God had prospered his store, and given him affluence; and for many years before his death, He gave him the more precious possession of divine grace. He had peculiarities, but they were all characterized by gracious feelings. In whatever else he may have been peculiar, I can testify from much knowledge of his private life, that he was peculiarly prayerful, peculiarly generous, and peculiarly attached to the promotion of the cause of Christ in Ireland. He had a strong feeling that it was wise for individuals to take separate divisions of the Lord's work; and although he never was in Ireland in his life, and knew very little about it, he often said that God had laid Ireland upon his heart. He had received the first effectual impulse to seek the salvation of Christ while listening to a charity sermon for an Irish object, from the late Rev. Henry Elliot, of Brighton, under whose ministry he afterwards rapidly grew in grace. This very small link with Irish interests, seems to have been the only means of turning his thoughts towards Ireland, by which he was made so importantly useful. "The hairs of your head are all numbered." Surely this was a very slender hair.

Having made such great progress in approaching, at least, towards the accomplishment of what had seemed impossible, I advanced cheerily on the next step. I went over to Dublin, and consulted with Miss Bellingham as to the further efforts to be made. The next point was to find some means of obtaining the names and addresses of a vast number of Roman Catholics and of Roman

Catholics only. This necessary limitation rendered all lists and directories useless, as not classifying the two religions. At last the thought occurred of engaging proper agents to travel through various parts of Ireland with some ostensible object in view, and with instructions to take down the names and addresses of Roman Catholics only, and enter them in a book, without giving these agents any intimation of the object in view. The Government had issued, in the beginning of 1845, a paper of inquiry concerning the state of the crops, and the nature of farming in Ireland. They wished this paper to be largely circulated. It was settled that a great number of these papers should be procured, and that the agents to be engaged should have the charge of distributing them in the districts to which they were sent.

Then came the difficulty of finding suitable agents, and this difficulty rose up only to be overcome. A good man, who had been a long time engaged as an agent of the old Dublin City Mission, was well known to Miss Bellingham. He was the first engaged. Through him three others were found. There had been a remarkable case of the conversion of a man who had been a student at Maynooth. He had been engaged as schoolmaster in a scriptural school in Dublin, at a very low salary; he was employed as another; and a sixth was added by an incidental circumstance. Thus I had six men—Protestants, and most of them converts, whom I engaged to journey mostly on foot, or from town to town on public cars, and to distribute the Government paper, making some inquiries in connection with it. But besides this, each agent was supplied with blank paper books, in which he was to write the name and address of as many Romanists of the respectable and middle class as he could. Each had also a number of postage stamps and envelopes; and when a certain number of pages were filled with names, he was to tear them out, put them in an envelope, and address it to me.

Then, too, I found the benefit of the experience of my past employment in foreign military service. I furnished each agent with a distinct route, *en militaire*, directing the lines of march through every one of the thirty-two counties of Ireland—the stages of their progress to be tested by the post-marks of their envelopes. By the end of August, 1845, the arrangement was complete, and the men were started on their commission.

Take difficulties in detail, and the impediments are greatly lessened; yet when you come face to face with each in order, it seems to be great. I calculated upon receiving thousands of addresses. How were they all to be written and arranged without a degree of publicity which would prevent the possibility of that secrecy which was essential to success? Knowing the Irish character, I counted much upon the magic of mystery, yet this would be impossible if many instruments were employed in producing the letters. Here again I see the finger of Providence—a hair that was numbered for the purpose had cast my lot in a small retired parish, and had drawn around me attached members of the congregation, who had been born of the Spirit under my ministry. Amongst these were some Christian young women whom I felt that I could trust. To these I explained enough to excite in them a lively interest, and I engaged them to write the addresses on stamped envelopes. As enclosures came from Ireland, I handed them over to those ladies, who, living a very retired life, had no difficulty in keeping their special occupation to themselves; and whose Christian wisdom so managed, that even the members of their own families were not acquainted with the object in view. Every day's post brought its supply of work for these ladies, and every week returned the tale of that work to the general depository.

For many years I had possessed a private printing press, which had been used originally for my own people only. It had grown to be more extensive, and had been handed over to a Christian young man, brought up under my own ministry. Clever and trustworthy, I could place entire reliance upon him. He had associated with him a printer whom he had himself instructed, and who, above that, had received the instruction of the Holy Spirit. These two carried on the whole of the process of printing the papers which were to be conveyed in the covers addressed by my indefatigable female helpers. In all, the number of persons in England who were in any way acquainted with the scheme amounted to seven, and every one of these were trustworthy spiritual Christians.

In the progress of this interesting work, the circumstances connected with the exhibition of the Holy Coat at Treves occurred, and the movement of Ronge and Czerski consequent upon it. This suggested the writing of another paper, which was entitled " A Look out of Ireland into Germany." As time passed on in the work of preparation new thoughts arose. I determined to get the "Voice from Heaven" translated into the Irish. Fanny Bellingham got this done for me in Dublin, and I had it printed in London. Then she suggested that the message to the Romanists would not be complete nor fit for a blessing unless it contained some portions of the Word of God. So a number of special and pointed texts were selected, and printed on a separate paper. Thus the contents of each envelope were, 1. "A Voice from Heaven to Ireland;" 2. The same in Irish; 3. "A Look out of Ireland into Germany;" and 4. A Paper of Selected Texts. These took the full of the money's worth for every penny envelope, though any overweight was carefully avoided.

By the end of the year 1845, about twenty thousand of these precious packets were made up, and addressed to so many Roman Catholics in every part of Ireland. An arrangement was then very carefully made for their simultaneous reception. The periods of postal delivery in the different districts of Ireland were ascertained. Bristol, Manchester, Birmingham, Liverpool, Edinburgh, and London were selected as the points of departure, and means were taken for having the letters posted in these places at such times as would secure the delivery of all the letters at all the places on the same day. Some of the distant districts required three days, some two, and others would be delivered on the day after being posted. The detail of all this was minutely arranged, and the numbers sent from the several places were so divided, that the excess need not retard any from one post-office.

When the whole was finally settled, the letters were packed in small divisions, each directed for its proper place. They were to go forth by the luggage-train from the neighbouring railway-station. A cart was brought to the door of the cottage in which the printing press was carried on. There is a little room in that cottage which had been the depository of the work as it grew to completion. It was now so filled with the closed parcels, that the whole floor was covered two layers thick with them. The whole of the seven persons who alone were in the secret assembled in that little room while the cart was waiting at the door. We all knelt down upon the very parcels which left us no other foot-room, and I solemnly delivered them to the Lord, entreating Him so to guide the way of each of those thousands of letters, that his own glory might be magnified in the salvation of the souls of unhappy Romanists, and that many might be brought "from darkness to light, and from the power of Satan to God." I feel sure that this prayer was echoed from the hearts of all the seven; the answer that has been vouchsafed let the records of the Irish Church Missions proclaim.

Wafted by this prayer, the parcels were put into the cart, and conveyed to their several starting points. The day on which the letters were delivered at the doors of those to whom they were addressed was the 16th of January, 1846. The record of the events of that day I will reserve for another chapter.

CHAPTER VII.

It was on the 16th of January, 1846, that the shower of letters fell like flakes of snow from heaven at the door of about twenty thousand Roman Catholics in every part of Ireland. Before proceeding to fulfil my promise of recording some of the events of that day, I must call special attention to that date. It is important to mark it, because a general feeling exists that the movement carried on through the Irish Church Missions took its rise from the effects of the famine. If this were the case, its origin could not but impart a certain character to its progress, and whatsoever fruits might result from time to time, permanent impulse could hardly be calculated upon. But this is not the case; a change was creeping over the spirit of the Romish peasants in Ireland, the dawn of which had been discernible for some years before the famine began. The harvests of 1843 and 1844 were splendid, so as to excite boastful expectations of high prosperity; and even in 1845, there were only such apprehensions as induced the Government to circulate the papers of instruction already referred to. The tokens of this change had been observed, and its progress watched during the previous years, and the efforts thus produced had time for organization and arrangement, and were matured for action by the close of 1845. The movement amongst the Romanists is of God. He had planted it, and it had taken root in the minds of the people long before. Then it was nurtured in blood; the awful famine of 1847, with its attendant horrors in 1848, worked wonderfully for its development. Thus it might almost be said that the movement gave a character to the famine, rather than that the famine characterized the movement; and while the mistaken impression would suggest the idea that the movement may be temporary, the true view of the case stamps it with the character of permanency. This makes it important to remember that the letters were delivered on the 16th January, 1846.

There was a natural anxiety to know the effect that would be produced, and circumstances were favourable for obtaining the information. The two ladies who had helped on the work were well acquainted with all the various agencies which were employed in every part of Ireland for spiritual service amongst the people. They had part in the several combinations that had been formed with similar objects, and were in communication with many Christian persons who were employing Scripture-Readers on their own account. I have a very interesting manuscript book which Miss Bellingham compiled for me at the very outset of our operations, in which is noted every spot in all Ireland where any efforts were then making to carry the light to the Romanists, with the names of all the parties engaged. She was felt to be a sympathizing heart, a centre to which they all instinctively turned in all the varied circumstances of their isolated work. We anticipated that many of them would spontaneously send accounts of what might happen without our giving any clue to the origin of the letters by making inquiries. Our anticipation was realized, but we scarcely expected the inundation of letters which poured in from almost every corner of the country. It appeared that the people were everywhere greatly stirred. They were taken by surprise, and were struck with the mysterious peculiarity of the event. That so many Romanists should receive the letter on the same day, and that no Protestant neighbour should get one, seemed to indicate that it must have been sent by some one who was well acquainted with each particular locality. The letters were accordingly read with peculiar attention. The portion in Irish puzzled many who could not read that language, and this led persons who had before shunned the Irish Scripture-Readers to go to them to get the paper read; and thus a friendly communication was opened with many Romanists who were afterwards led to read the Scriptures.

The effect was of course various with various people, and in different places, but in general the result was an anxiety to possess the papers, a serious impression that there was much that was true in them, and a desire to inquire further, and to know more. The conduct of the priests varied in different localities. The communications from the north say that the priests were in general quiet, and endeavoured to obtain the papers from the people by fair means, though with expressions of disapprobation. The persons who wrote from the south and west, and from some parts of Louth and Cavan, gave account of great violence on the part of the priests, and strong efforts to prevent any one from keeping or reading the papers; yet multitudes of instances were given in which the people either resisted or evaded the priests' command, and retained their letters.

It is quite impossible to convey to the mind of the reader anything like an adequate idea of the general excitement that was produced, and which was continued for a time, as the extent of the letters became known through the communications between friends in distant parts of the country. The people in Cork and Kerry found that those in Donegal and Derry had the same letters on the same day. Dublin and Galway, Louth and Limerick, distant and divided districts, all alike favoured in the same manner, at the same time, and with the same distinction of creed. This kept the excitement alive, and left a wondering expectation on the minds of the people looking for what was to come of so strange a matter. Though no clear impression can be given by a few specimens of the communications received, yet it may be well to show the nature of these accounts by inserting two or three of the letters written by persons who gave the information without suspecting that they were communicating with the author of the letters. It is difficult to select from the large number that were forwarded to me, but almost at hazard I take the following :—

From the County of Donegal.

Feb. 14, 1846.—I have been very uneasy that I could not have written to you sooner, and in particular to let you know about a vast number of anonymous letters which are in circulation among the Romanists of this part of the country, and have even met with some of them in G. also. I have to let you know that the minds of many of them in this part are much agitated by these letters; but I am happy to remark that they have laid the foundation of many useful conversations I hope, in my travels among the people; and I have reason to hope and believe they will be the means of raising a spirit of inquiry among many of them, which may be blessed to the breaking off those tyrannical chains by which they are so strongly bound by these cunning and crafty Italian policemen, who are daily lying in wait to deceive; and it may yet come to pass that these letters may be acknowledged by some of them to be what they are represented to be—that is, "a voice from heaven." Dear lady, I think it necessary to let you know that these letters came to the country in the beginning of the week, which gave the people an opportunity of having a week's perusal of them, before the priests had time to have them published in the chapels, as the priests did not neglect doing so on the following Sunday. This they have done (I am informed) with the wisdom of the serpent, by making as light of these letters as possible, telling the people to light their pipes with them, which I am certain many of them may do; but I am convinced this will not be general; and I have reason to think they have kindled a fire in the hearts of some, which will never be quenched by the powers of darkness.

From the County of Cork.

Jan. 30, 1846.—There are some most excellent tracts sent through the post to several quarters of Ireland. They are causing great noise. The priests are furious about the matter, and the Popish press also; but the people read them: and I have *every reason to hope* they will do incalculable good. The priests order whoever receive them to bring them to themselves without reading; but I have heard some of them say they "would not give them to priest or minister;" they are very happily written.

From the County of Kerry.

Feb. 25, 1846.—I had three letters from different parts of the country, asking me if I could get any of these *English* letters, to send them by post, for that they had seen some with a *pedlar* who sold them at *threepence each*. Very many got them that do not own to them, so as not to have the priest come to hear it.

While these communications afforded abundant proof that a powerful impulse to inquiry had been given, it was important to ascertain the state of feeling by personal observation, and I undertook more than one journey to Ireland with this view. Everything that I saw and heard in these visits, tended to confirm the impression produced by the information I had received. It was in the course of these visits that I first went to Castelkerke, where the Providence of God opened the way for the first direct Missionary efforts. I found there an open door for making the experiment which would test the principle I had so strongly pressed upon my clerical brethren, and which they had so strongly opposed; and I entered into it the more readily because I felt the necessity for having some ostensible reason to assign to my friends in England for my otherwise unexplained absences from home. The story of the Castelkerke Mission must have a chapter to itself; and attention to the chronological order of its events must not interrupt the narrative of those efforts of which I have yet only related the first.

It was important that the interest excited by the letters of the 16th January should be kept alive. There were many names on the original lists which had not been taken into the first flight of letters. It was determined that a second issue of letters should be sent, in which these should be included with as many of the former as possible. The experience I had gained in my recent inquiries gave me the clue to the subject of which to treat, and a tract came forth, entitled "Irishmen's Rights." It showed that every Irishman had a right to read the Scriptures; and it explained that the rule of the Church of Rome does not positively deny this right, but requires that nobody should read them without the permission of a priest, and it advised the people to go to the priests and ask for such permission.

This suggested another step in the work; a letter was drawn up to the priests; the Catholic directory supplied the names and addresses of all the priests in Ireland, and this letter, accompanied by chosen extracts from the Douay version of the New Testament, was sent by post to every one of them, Regular and Secular. This letter was as follows :—

REVEREND SIR,—You are respectfully requested to give serious consideration to the following argument, concerning which your practical opinion may shortly be called for.

You are no doubt aware, that it is by a mistake that the Protestants assert that the reading of the Bible is absolutely prohibited by the Roman Catholic doctrines.

You are also aware, that the true state of the case is, that the laity are forbidden to read any version of the Holy Scriptures, without ecclesiastical authority first had and obtained in the form of a written permission from the priest.

The priest is thus constituted the judge of the propriety of granting such permission in each particular case, and of conceding to any individual of his flock such licence to read the Holy Scriptures in whole or in part, as to him may seem right. While, therefore, the reading of the Scriptures by the laity is restrained and limited, not only is no restraint or limit imposed upon the priest, as regards his own reading of the Bible, but it is distinctly required of each priest that he should make himself acquainted with the Holy Scriptures; in order to be able to form a judgment, whether they may be safely read, in whole or in part, by any individual of his flock who may apply to him for such a permission as he is authorized to grant.

It being thus plainly the duty of every priest of the Roman Catholic Church to read the Holy Scriptures himself, you are respectfully asked—Have *you* read the Holy Scriptures?

If not the whole, have you at least read the New Testament?

Have you read it in the original Greek? or, should this be difficult to you, have you read the Latin Vulgate?

Have you made yourself acquainted with the versions in English and in Irish, which are those likely to be found in the hands of your flock?

If this should not be the case, it is respectfully suggested to you, that you should apply yourself to such reading at once; or how could you be capable of forming a judgment, in case any of your flock should exercise this undoubted right of asking your permission to read the Scriptures, upon such reasonable grounds as no honest man ought to refuse to consider?

Suppose a dozen or twenty respectable Roman Catholics, such as farmers, or tradesmen, or gentlemen, living in your parish, were to ask such a permission from you, what reason could you give for refusing, if you had never read the Scriptures yourself? It is by no means unlikely that such an application may be made to you by even a greater number than a dozen or twenty.

In the letter to the people enclosing the tract called "Irishmen's Rights," it was stated that the priest of the parish had "lately had a friendly letter sent to him, respectfully reminding his Reverence of his duty to read the Bible himself," a copy of this letter to the priest was enclosed, and the person was told that according to the rules of the Church of Rome anybody may read the Book of God, if he has got a permission under the hand of a priest. To enable the person who received the letter to act on this rule two things were added in the same cover; one was a permission to search the Scriptures, signed by "A True Priest," the other was a single leaf of the New Testament in English and another in Irish. This was said to be "a drop of the water of life;" and it was added, "it seems a pity to tear up a Bible on purpose, but all the leaves shall go for a shower of drops amongst you, all over Ireland; whatever leaf you chance to get, you can go to your neighbour, and see whether his leaf comes next, and so you may help one another by putting your drops together."

My unwearied helpers set to work with ready zeal, and we got together sixteen thousand of these letters; they were not sent on one day as before, but in divisions as they were ready. They were posted mostly in Edinburgh and London, and were received in the months of August and September, 1846. The permission was as follows:—

PERMISSION BY AUTHORITY.

This is to certify that the Blessed Lord Himself gives you, Mr. ——, full and free permission and commandment to "Search the Scriptures" (John v. 39), in the language you understand; and I would advise you as a friend, lest the Lord should judge you and punish you for neglect of his Word, to take the Bible and search it, and to try if I am telling you the truth, for He has laid it upon me to send this permission to you.

I am, your Friend, and
A TRUE PRIEST.

The result of this issue threw great light upon the effect produced by the former letters; many persons took care to say nothing about what they had received, and this was evidently with a desire to prevent the papers from being taken from them; they had profited by experience. Many, on the other hand, refused to receive them, and they were returned to the post-office unopened, and so the contents became well known. Communications from friends were received relating to this new issue, as upon the former occasion. The following specimen will be enough to convey a just impression of the general tone of all the accounts from every quarter.

From the County of Kerry.

Oct. 16, *Monday.*—I proceeded to U——, where I met some acquaintances, who told me of a great stir among the people there, caused by their receiving a second draft of letters from England. During the evening, fell into conversation with three schoolmasters who live in that locality, each of whom got a letter. Told me they took up this subject, and discussed it several nights with the farmers of that neighbourhood, who also got letters. They said the country about them is all on fire. Priest T—— is doing all he can to quench it, by fulminating curses against those who refuse burning those letters. The people often tell him he should rather point out what is wrong in them, which he has failed to do; so the people are beginning to see the side truth lies.

Wednesday.—Went to M——, where I visited the place of another farmer. I asked him if he had any news. He said the place all about him was in a state of rebellion for the last fortnight; and every day people are getting worse, talking about religion. In the evening, called at the house of a neighbouring farmer, where twenty-seven persons collected; and one young man, more learned than the rest, was explaining the letter in Irish.

Thursday.—Visited a shopkeeper in P——; told me that scarcely a night passes that people are not disputing about their right to read the Bible; and that all this was brought on by nonsensical letters. He says he wonders the priest is not able to put an end to such ugly work, before the people be pulling out each others' eyes.

Friday.—Visited A——, where I met two Irish scholars, who told me the names of about twenty farmers who got those letters, and found they are giving this subject their attentive consideration.

All these operations, resulting from the ascertained effects of the letters of the 16th

January, 1846, bring us to the end of September in the same year, and it will not be thought that any time had been lost when the smallness of the instrumentality, the necessity for secrecy, and the difficulties in the way are taken into consideration. But the large amount of the success attending the first effort, had encouraged us to expect still more, and the following steps were promptly taken in October. These require a new chapter for their explanation.

CHAPTER VIII.

THE last chapter brought the Story of the Irish Church Missions down to October, 1846. The encouragement of the previous part of the year, and the many openings which had been unexpectedly developed by which to ascertain the state of the Irish Roman Catholic mind, made new arrangements necessary in order to take advantage of these great opportunities. It should be remembered that the object in view, in these early plans, was not the formation of any separate machinery such as God's Providence has since been pleased to create. The object was to produce such a plain and extensive manifestation of the real state of the Irish mind, as would convince those incredulous brethren who have been already referred to, and excite them to a combined and energetic effort for the conversion of the Romanists. This should be kept in mind in tracing out the steps which were taken.

With this view, I addressed a letter to the "Morning Herald" on the 11th of October, 1846, on the "Real State of Ireland," which was admitted into their columns, and produced at least so much attention as led to a second letter in the following December. A short extract from the former of these letters will give a condensed view of what was considered at that time to be the condition of people's minds; and subsequent experience has fully justified the opinions thus expressed. They were as follows :—

The lower classes of the Irish people are at this moment, for the most part, in a state of mind, with respect to the Roman Catholic religion, quite different from that willing bondage which has so long been the prominent characteristic of their adherence. It is not that they are more disposed to regard Protestantism with favour, neither can it be said that they are less superstitiously influenced by what may be called the spell of Romish rites, under a feeling which they imbibed at the breast, and which has swayed them all their lives. The evidence that these are abiding habits of mind arises on every occasion of intercourse with the Romish peasants of Ireland. But while such feelings still hold their power in a very great degree, the agents by whom these were formerly wielded as instruments of unresisted despotism have come to be regarded in a very different manner, so that the poor bewildered creatures seem to be in a state of much confusion of mind. The magic spell of Romanism is not broken from them; but the magicians cannot pronounce the incantations with effective power. Stations are performed at holy wells as of old; but the confession, which involves contact with the priest, is put off by every possible device. The sacred vestments are as awful as ever; but those who wear them are despised and hated.

Two great classes of causes have acted from different quarters upon the Irishman's mind. The priests themselves have set one class in motion—their tyranny had long been felt and submitted to; but the outrageous intensity of bitterness with which a large proportion of the priesthood have, for the last few years more especially, used their prerogative of *cursing*, has been one main means of disgusting the whole heart of the people; and thus they have become more capable of forming a considerate judgment concerning the disgraceful immorality that marks the lives of too many of the priests, particularly in the more remote districts. Then, too, not a few priests have taxed the credulity of their blind flocks too far; while pretending to confer benefits of various kinds miraculously, the failures have been so gross as to concur in awakening the dormant powers of reason. When a man, under the direction of his priest, has sprinkled holy water on the thatch of his cabin in a violent storm, expecting the wind to pay due respect to the blessing which had given such power to the water—and has found the straws scattered to the heavens in spite of the charm—he not only has recourse to bands and weights to secure his roof upon the next occasion of danger, but he becomes disposed to join his neighbours in despising the boast of the priest's power. And when the same charmed holy water has been used by the priest's own hands over the withering stalk of the potato, and yet the root yields nothing but a mass of corruption for the famishing dupe, no wonder that the heart-broken man shrinks from the deceiving miracle-mongers. These things have been done—the latter in several instances—and it is not to be doubted that they have contributed something towards the breaking of the spell of priestcraft: although it is certainly true that the inveterate credulity of a large number of Romanists is proof against even this.

But perhaps the most effectual of the causes connected with the priests themselves, is the unfeeling rapacity with which the dues are drawn from those who are in the extremest poverty. The affections of the poor people have been made a source of profit in a manner which has tended to dry up the current of them. In such cases, the superstitious credulity of warmly affectionate hearts clashes with their deep, even starving poverty, and in the collision the prestige of the priesthood is crushed.

While gathering the intelligence of the results produced by "Irishmen's Rights," and the letter to the priests, it became a serious question what would be the best mode of bringing out tangible evidence of the state we believed to exist, without at the same time dispelling the mystery of our secret? It was proposed that suitable and trustworthy agents should be employed to journey into various parts of Ireland, to make special inquiries, converse openly with the people on controversial subjects, and make full reports of all that passed under their own eyes. To carry out this plan to anything like an adequate extent, and with proper efficacy, would require two things not easily to be obtained. The amount of means that would be necessary would very far exceed what had been already employed. Mr. Durant never lacked liberality, but the exercise of it was always poised with prudence. I could not ask him to give so large a sum as my plan required; but I thought it a right time to confer with him on the propriety of entrusting our secret to some few selected Christian men of large heart and large means, proposing to them a share of the burden of these experimental expenses.

With his consent, I conferred with some half-dozen excellent friends. The marvellous success of the last two months set the matter in a very different light from what it would have taken two years before. They responded liberally, and sufficient funds were raised to carry out the next portion of the plan.

But the second difficulty was by far the greater. Where were to be found the suitable agents for so delicate a work? There were many searchings, many testings, several journeys to Ireland, several individuals brought to England for personal inspection. At length, or rather with much greater rapidity than could have been the case had not the Providence of God again and again exemplified his own word that the hairs of our head are all numbered, eight persons were chosen. It cannot be said that the same amount of confidence was felt towards each and all of these; but while in some I had full confidence, I had a feeling that I could depend upon all.

They were called Messengers, and they were sent forth two and two, so classed that there should be always one of more age and experience than his companion. All Ireland was divided into four Routes, and each pair of Messengers had his appointed direction.

A map of the country was given to each, the places where they were to sojourn for a season were marked down, the number of days they were to remain, the periods when their reports were to be sent in; all these were distinctly stated.

When all was ready, the eight Messengers met in Dublin; it was a solemn occasion when they were assembled to be dismissed to their several missions. The few words addressed to them seemed to fall upon their hearts, and to prepare them for the earnest prayer with which they were sent forth to their work. It was a moment not to be forgotten; the remembrance is deeply affecting, especially since it has been seen how much precious fruit God has brought forth from that little seed, and how very far his purpose then exceeded the limit of our most sanguine expectations.

In order to convey a just notion of the work of these Messengers, some extracts must be given from the special instructions which were placed in their hands for their guidance:—

INSTRUCTIONS FOR THE MESSENGERS.

May the Holy Spirit of God direct the mind in suggesting these instructions, and enable those who act upon them to do all things to the glory of the name of Jesus Christ.

1. The object in view is to strive, by all holy means, to dispel the darkness and ignorance from the minds of Irish Romanists. This is to be done by lifting up Christ and Him crucified alone, and by urging the Romanists to try every part of the system under which they are bound, by the Scriptures, and by the Scriptures alone; and for this purpose, the practical exhortation must tend to make them read or hear read the Book of God as a duty and a right. This may be summed up thus:—The one object—the spiritual emancipation of Irish Romanists; the essential means—the proclaiming of Christ's salvation; the leading them to search the Scriptures.

2. Whatever course in detail may be pointed out by Providential circumstances, these principles must never be departed from; the mind of the Messenger must be directed to them singly, simply, and at all times.

4. In the necessary and bold exposure of the abominations of Romanism, a tender and charitable care must be observed with respect to all expressions that may apply with personality to Romanists. Our blessed Lord's distinction

between the sinner and the sin must always be the model. Hopeful compassion should mark all expressions that relate to the persons; uncompromising faithfulness should characterize the denouncing of the thing.

8. Whenever the question is asked of the Messengers, Whence they come? Why they come? or, Who sent them? etc., etc., the answer must substantially be this: God sends us; his Providence has opened the way; anybody and everybody is bound to stretch out a hand to save a perishing soul; we simply tell you to read the Bible—to look to Christ. There needs no authority for doing this; everybody who has read the Bible ought to do the same toward anybody who has not. If the Bible justify us, it does not signify who we happen to be, or who happen to be our helpers.

12. The Messengers must endeavour to be exceedingly quiet in their first efforts, carefully avoiding all unnecessary display; while they with equal care avoid the slightest appearances of want of Christian boldness in maintaining their principles. Quietness without fear, courage without a boast, watchfulness in employing private opportunities, boldness when publicity becomes necessary—these should characterize the conduct of the Messengers.

18. Every Messenger must remember that the least occasion for scandal in him will effectually mar the work. This thought must regulate his conduct with the most scrupulous exactness. He must never allow a debt of the most trifling amount to be justly charged against him in his journeyings from place to place; and he must be careful not to receive obligations from people beyond the proper limits of kind hospitality.

19. Having such a work, in such a world, with such enemies, difficulties must be anticipated, both such as are connected with failure, and such as are connected with success. The results may be very painful, and even dangerous; but serving such a Master, with such promises, and such a

reward, we may rest assured that He who has the ordering of all things will supply the courage to support every danger, and arrange all events for the good of his servants. On Him must all dependence be placed.

20. And now these dear servants of the Lord engaged in this special work for God's glory, and the salvation of their countrymen's souls—these soldiers of Christ, are solemnly committed to the care and direction of the great Captain of our salvation; with the humble petition that they may be filled with the Spirit of power, and of love, and of a sound mind; that they may be strengthened and supported in every step of their way by the power of the Holy Ghost; and blessed with the fullest success, to the glory of the name of Christ Jesus the Lord. Amen.

It was the winter of 1846-7 that broke the heart of all Ireland; and it was the dreary length of the year 1847-8 which scattered the corpses of her children over the land. The combined horrors of famine are inconceivable to those who have never felt or seen them. I have witnessed the desolation of war, I have ministered in the death-chambers of general pestilence; I can, therefore, estimate the comparative anguish caused by these sore judgments of God. Nothing is comparable to famine. It seems as though the whole man, the requirements of his body, the thoughts of his mind, the feelings of his heart, were all placed together in a crucible, and melted down by the fiery trial of famine into a mad craving for food, with strong yearnings, powerless through weakness. If the natural love of a mother for her offspring could yield to this all-powerful solvent, no wonder that the inbred superstitions of Roman teaching could also be reduced. In this way the preparation already made by God for the reception of his divine teaching was facilitated by the fearful judgment spread over the land. The untold amount of sympathy and succour which rolled over the channel from Protestant England, and was administered and distributed for the most part with uninquiring impartiality by the Protestant clergy, dropped upon the melting hearts of starving Romanists thus prepared, and greatly helped to bridge over the broad chasm which so long impeded the approach of Protestant Christians to their Romanist neighbours.

It was in the midst of all these circumstances that the Messengers were sent to execute their difficult task. They were sent forth in October, 1846, and between that time and the spring of 1847 I made several journeys to Ireland, suddenly and unexpectedly appearing at the points at which the Messengers ought to be found according to their instructions. In each of these visits they were taken by surprise, but in no one instance did I find them neglecting their duty. My object was to test their work and the strict correctness of their Reports; and the result was so satisfactory, that I felt strong in the capacity which these visits gave me of being able to testify to the general accuracy of the accounts furnished by the large body of Reports which were regularly received. It would be too long to supply any adequate selections from these Reports, the whole of which communicated full confirmation of the views already put forth on this subject.

On my return from a visit to Ireland, soon after Christmas, 1846, I felt strongly that an occasion was afforded for directing the minds of the people with reference to the effects of the famine, which were already severely felt from the failure of the harvest. Another tract was therefore written, entitled "The Food of Man;" its object was to draw out the power of that truth, "Man shall not live by bread alone, but by every word that proceedeth from God;" and it went on to show, that as the priests had cursed the food which God had provided for the soul, God had withdrawn his blessing from that which he usually supplied for the body. The secret machinery worked by my earnest helpers was set in motion; and early in the year 1847 another flight of letters was despatched. This contained the tract called "The Food of Man;" and the weight was filled up by another tract, which gave an account of a trial at the Antrim assizes, at Carrickfergus, on the 20th of March, 1846, in which a priest, the Rev. Luke Walsh, was condemned in £70 damages and the costs, for having cursed by bell, book, and candle one Charles McLaughlin, for having taught his neighbour to read the Scriptures in the Irish language. A slip on which were printed several extracts from the Douay version of the New Testament was added to make up the pennyworth of postage.

Several circumstances connected with these letters had the effect of reviving the mystery of the former ones. A large number of new names had been collected, and therefore not a few received these letters who had not received the former. Some persons to whom these were addressed had died, and their letters were eagerly handed about, read, and sought for; while a larger number than before were careful to prevent the priest from knowing that they had received them. The Messengers had had no intimation of the intended effort, but they speedily found the effects of it in every one of their districts, and their Reports conveyed constant communications of the results. The year 1847 developed much more of the preparation for the great work which was to be accomplished, and it will require another chapter to open the course of those events to the reader. Before, however, this is attempted, we must go back, and take up that branch of the Story of the Irish Church Missions which was planted at Castelkerke. To this our next chapter shall be devoted.

CHAPTER IX.

We have been tracing the Story of the Irish Church Missions in the regular course of events, leading on to the crisis of their organization as a Society. In doing this we have travelled, as it were, along the main line without attention to any collateral branch. Having now brought the reader to what may be considered a station, at the end of the year 1846, we must go back a little in time, and give some account of an important part of the work, which providentially opened at Castelkerke.

It will be remembered, that shortly after the distribution of the letters on the 16th January, 1846, I had made several journeys to Ireland to ascertain the effect that had been produced. I had before visited Galway and Oughterard, and Miss Bellingham had given me a letter of introduction to a retired officer and his lady, who had gone to reside on a small property on the shores of Lough Corrib. There is a castle in the midst of the lake, and a cottage on the summit of a lovely hill, which the proprietor was transforming into a comfortable mansion. A scattered population on this property and around the shores of the lake numbered at that time about 2000; and the characteristic increase of the families of Irish peasants, made it more than probable that one-fourth of that number were children. I have described the beauty of the features of this spot in another work, and I will not occupy these pages with the repetition.

While the gentleman was occupied in transforming the desolation of Doon Hill into a habitation of taste and comfort, his wife was stirred at the sight of the ignorant children abounding in the district. She gathered a few girls together in a cottage to teach them to read, and was encouraged in her early efforts. The rector of the parish, the Rev. E. L. Moore, was a man of Christian earnestness. His church and residence were thirteen miles off, at Cong, but he readily gave her every assistance in his power. In the midst of many labours he contrived to go on a week-day once a fortnight, to have divine service with the family, and to examine the little handful of children. He did more, for he set forward a subscription among his friends, for the purpose of building a small school-house, which, by the assistance of the proprietor, soon took such a form, that though it could not be said to be completed, was a gathering-place which might be called the school-house.

Matters were in this state when I first visited Castelkerke. I was warmly received. It needed but little intercourse to discover the Christian earnestness of the excellent lady. It was also easy to perceive that her husband was proud of this earnestness and of its results. I could not help feeling that I had been led providentially to Castelkerke by the drawing of one of those hairs which are all numbered; and I made up my mind that this would be a point from which future active aggressive work might be effectively carried on. I offered to adopt the work which had been thus begun, to undertake the finishing of the school-house, and to give them all the assistance I could, provided they understood that I should address myself plainly and openly to the Romanists, to instruct them in the truth of the gospel in contrast with the falsehoods of Rome; to this they heartily consented.

When I returned to England I related all this to Mr. Durant, and I expected that he would give the means for completing the Castelkerke school-house. I was somewhat surprised, and not a little disappointed, when he objected to give money for the purpose. We were not sufficiently advanced in our main object. It was not wise to expend our means on brick and mortar, etc., etc. Mr. Durant was most systematic as a man of business, clear-headed and cautious. This renders the course he took in the beginning of the matter the more remarkable, as more evidently directed by the finger of God. I found that he did not wish to contribute to the smaller details which I laid before him, while he kept his eye steadily on the grand point in view. It will be seen that at a subsequent period he became sensible of the importance of detail; but at this time I felt it wise not to press him on the subject.

Considerable difficulty was thus produced; but I was brought up from a child in the constant repetition of those lines, by which my father sought to mould my character— .

> The wise and active conquer difficulties
> By daring to attempt them. Folly and sloth
> Shiver and shrink at sight of toil and trouble,
> And make the impossibility they fear.

So instead of giving up the plan for Castelkerke, I prayed, and felt that the Providence which took me there had an object in view— the hair was numbered for that special use, and I determined to open a little mission fund for Castelkerke, and to bring it before the class of Christians who are able and willing to give their pounds, though they are not able, though they would be willing, to give their hundreds.

I put forth a little tract, detailing some of the matters at Castelkerke, and it pleased God to give it success. Money was gradually contributed, and the work went on. Tract after tract followed, till six were sent forth during the time of the famine in 1847 and 1848. But at a very early period of this effort, I became sensible that the arrangements of Providence were wiser and better than my plans. While at the end of 1846 there was a widespread feeling of interest with reference to the anticipated famine, it was general and diffusive. There was a need of some special and defined point round which the rays of Christian sympathy might cluster. And as regards myself, there needed some ostensible object of which I could speak, to account for my many visits to Ireland. The interesting case of Castelkerke, though too small to produce anything like a general feeling, yet it operated in that direction; and as regards myself, it was precisely the object that was wanted. Mr. Durant, though he did not contribute, became interested in my little mission, and watched my operations there with cautious attention.

I visited Castelkerke from time to time, and on each occasion I had encouraging tokens that the work would not be in vain; the parents of the children came freely whenever a notice was given that there was to be preaching in the school-house; that schoolhouse had been finished, but the manner in which it was crowded, and the number of people who stood round the windows, made it necessary to enlarge it; and as funds gradually came in, and the kind proprietor was ever ready to afford help by the gift of material, the school-house was enlarged; and when I have been preaching there, I have seen a hundred and fifty souls, old and young, crammed into its walls. The approaching famine, which desolated the country in 1847, was seen as a heavy cloud in the horizon at the close of 1846, and the thought was suggested of procuring funds to afford relief to the little children who came to the Castelkerke school; a channel was thus open, through which the streams of charity flowed, to maintain many souls within the reach of gospel salvation, who would otherwise have passed out of the body in their spiritual darkness.

Through my kind friends in Dublin, the Ladies' Auxiliary of the Irish Society lent their assistance in procuring the means of supporting an Irish Scripture-Reader among the people, and some of my own flock in England delighted to consider this as a special mission from amongst themselves, and contributed to maintain a school-master at Castelkerke. Amongst the ties that will be traced out in the great day of the Lord as having been formed during the preparatory period upon earth, a powerful though secret link will be discovered to have existed between these two spots, formed at the throne of grace, and strengthened by the abiding interest that flows from oft-repeated prayer.

I need not detail the events of the several visits I paid to Castelkerke, some of which are amongst the most interesting and affecting incidents of the whole story; many of these are set forth in the little tracts which were issued occasionally to obtain contributions to the funds. The tracts were afterwards condensed into a volume which was largely circulated; and as the events they relate bear importantly on the Irish Church Missions, some of them must be recorded here. These can be best related as they were at first set forth, with all the freshness of their recent occurrence. The following extracts from the volume entitled "Castelkerke," will give specimens of the work there carried on :—

How great was the difference between the events of this visit and that which took place early in 1846, and gave rise to the first little tract. *Then* an unfinished school-room contained its thirty-six scholars ; *now* a school-room finished, and besides considerably enlarged, was filled with a hundred and fifty children—many brought over by the new boat built for the purpose. *Then* a few people hardly ventured to run the risk of being present at the Protestant service ; *now* a crowd of willing and ready hearers filled every corner. *Then* they gave a doubtful attention to a dreaded gospel; *now* an attentive ear was given to the word that seemed to be thirsted for.

The hearty welcome of the comparatively few people who lived on the Castelkerke side was cheering on the Saturday of my arrival; and close inquiry from the Schoolmaster and the Scripture-Reader fully confirmed the encouraging reports I had received from the kind and judicious friends who live amongst the people. It appeared that the next day would be a testing time for many; as, besides the service I intended to have in the school-room, it happened to be the third Sunday since the last Mass was said in the neighbourhood; and therefore, having Mass only one Sunday in three, those who were truly Romanists in feeling would be drawn to the Mass-house; while another class would be drawn by another attraction to the same locality, though not for the same purpose. A faction-fight had been appointed to take place after Mass, near the spot where Mass was said. A faction-fight is happily a thing unknown in England; and it requires more knowledge of the manners and customs of the people of Galway than can be conveyed in this letter, to give any other notion than will arise from its name. The opposing parties had agreed to meet this Sunday, and fight out their feud; a circumstance that was sure to draw a number of idlers to the spot. The fight, however, as I afterwards learned, did not take place, though it was fully believed that it would. Against these attractions, the school-house at Castelkerke contended successfully. It was so filled with adults, that the children gave up their forms, and crowded, or rather huddled together, almost one upon the other, in the open space that had been left before the desk. Upwards of a hundred and sixty adults, and a hundred and forty-seven children, all Romanists, occupied the room, and listened with eager attention to the prayers, to the reading of the Scriptures, and to the sermon which I preached to them. It was the simple gospel, and spoken in as simple words as I could use. I believe that they understood me generally. At the end of the sermon I determined to act upon the information I had received as to their state of mind with regard to Romanism, from which I was told they were loosened in so great a degree. I told them that I was quite aware of the various motives that were influencing them—the effect of the *stir-about* which had been given them there for the famine, and the possible hope of future benefit which they might imagine. But I warned them of the danger to their souls of deceit and double-dealing—of the single-heartedness that God looked for—of the bold confession of Christ that He requires—of the effectual working of the Holy Spirit. Then I pointed out the folly of attempting to serve God and mammon—the impossibility of entering into the kingdom of heaven through a time-serving profession of faith, holding at the same time the false notion of the sacrifice of the Mass. After this, I asked them whether, if I should be able to obtain for them a regular ministry in their own Irish tongue, they were willing to form themselves into a regular congregation to attend it—separating themselves from the bondage of that yoke of falsehood which had so long enslaved them, and seeking to be admitted, through the knowledge of Christ, into the glorious liberty of the children of God. I bid all who felt thus, to hold up their hands. The movement amongst the people that followed this, suggested to my mind the thought that there was not a perfect understanding of the token I appointed. Though a good many hands were raised, there was an appearance of indecision, which might arise from backwardness of feeling, or from uncertainty of comprehension. To settle this, I subsequently repeated what I had said; and directed the Irish Scripture-Reader to interpret it in their own language. He bid those amongst them who consented, to hold up their hands; and then followed instantly a prompt and decided movement. Every arm was raised, without the slightest appearance of the inquiring look that had produced the pause upon the previous occasion.

One of the most encouraging tokens which led me to hope for great results in this place, was the remarkable preparedness of feeling in all the surrounding neighbourhood. The following extracts from "Castelkerke" will show this :—

On Sunday evening I had a long and interesting conversation with some of the communicants (of whom ten converts partook of the Lord's Supper that day). One of them spoke of the great desire to learn the truth, and to hear the Scriptures, which was manifested by the people at Glan, a populous district on the shores of Lough Corrib, about six miles off. He spoke so largely of the willingness of his neighbours, and of their readiness to send their children to him to be taught the Word of God, that I asked him whether he could give me a proof of it, if I went myself amongst them. He seemed delighted at the thought, and assured me that any day he would get me a house full of people, by telling them that I would preach the gospel to them. "Suppose I took you at your word, and went to-morrow," said I. "Indeed, now, your reverence should not find a better day; for it's tomorrow itself when the two priests come from Oughterard, and have called a station to confess the people, in the very house that is the next to my own; and then we would see who would come to the gospel, and who would go to the priests."

There were several present who thought it would be "too hard upon the crathurs to try them so close. Wouldn't they be afraid, though they might have it in their hearts to come?" "Sure that's the very thing we would find out," said the man of Glan. "Is not it our Lord Himself that says, 'Whosoever shall be ashamed of Me now, I will be ashamed of him in that day'?"

I was of the same mind with this good man, and asked the hour when the priests would come. They were to be in the village by nine, and might leave it by eleven. "Then I'll be there at ten," said I, "to be sure not to miss the right time." This was agreed. The weather began to lower, and the time to be late. The lake lay between these good people and their homes; and my friend from Glan had to announce my coming by the early morning. So I dismissed them with a blessing, which I felt to receive, in praying that it might be imparted.

The next morning we were up long before the December sun. My friends had prepared a six-oared boat. The Scripture-Reader went with me to show me the way; and the Castelkerke Schoolmaster begged so hard to join the party, that arrangements were made for the purpose. While we continued in the long arm of the lake we made our way rapidly; but when we passed into the broad expanse, the wind was directly against us, and an hour's hard rowing had not enabled us to make half the way we expected for the time. We had to round a long tongue of land which stretched its promontory far into the lake; and at last it began to be hopeless to expect that we could arrive by ten o'clock. "If I know the map, we might get to Glan in a short walk over that promontory," said I. "Two bits of miles will take you there," was the reply. "Then row into the bay as quick as you can." We were presently on shore, and making our way across the boggy land to find the "starvation road" by which I had come; and when we had reached it, we found cabins dotting the land as we went along. Two or three men came out from some of these, and greeted me at once with the *Ceade mille falthur* blessing; they joined our little party, and were joined by others further on, until the snowball gathering made a goodly band of some twenty people as we approached the village.

"We must be near to the priests," said I, "for these two women that are coming with their beads in their hands look very much like a pair of penitents." "Sure they are," said one, "and just come from confession; and you'll see the house before you are face to face with the women."

Sure enough in a few steps, upon turning a corner, we

saw the house, but we never had the opportunity of being face to face with the women; for the sight of us made them avert their looks with evident dismay; and keeping at the very verge of the way's breadth, they muttered their "Hail Maries" as we passed them. We met some other women, coming in the same direction and from the same work, but no men, and the women were but few.

About twenty yards from the house where the priests held the station, and immediately at the bottom of the rising ground on which it stood, was the cabin of my convert friend, where for some time he has kept a little Scriptural school, and in which he had now collected a congregation of his neighbours. On my arrival, he slipped the door off its hinges, and laid it down as a bridge over a considerable puddle which was characteristically near the entrance. I made my way into a place that contained a condensed mass of human beings. As the light only came through the door, all I could see when I went in was a range of faces so crowded together, that it was difficult to imagine how the bodies could be stowed. Looking over the front rank into the dark recess beyond, I asked whether there was anybody behind them? And the correct reply was, "Sure all the crathurs are crushed in the corner."

I offered up an earnest prayer, and spoke in simple words to these poor Romanists. I told them of Christ—his love—his salvation. I seized the opportunity of making the experiment of teaching them through an interpreter. Endeavouring to accommodate my English to the Irish phraseology and tone of mind, I spoke in short sentences; and I bid the Reader whom I had brought with me to turn every third or fourth sentence into Irish. The plan appeared to be thoroughly successful. Gazing with fixed attention, they seemed to catch the sense, and to feel it. I pressed on them the constant and earnest use of that little powerful prayer, which has already been blessed in so many ways, and to so many people; and having taken pains to be correct in my pronunciation, I repeated it to them in Irish, "O God, for Christ's sake, give me the Holy Spirit." As soon as I had spoken this, a man in the crowd addressed me in Irish. He had, however, hardly uttered a sentence, before there was quite a clamour in the cabin; many voices were directed to the man. My knowledge of Irish was not enough to enable me to understand all this, and I applied to my interpreter, who told me that, upon my speaking Irish, the man began to beg of me; and as soon as his object was perceived by the others, they all bid him desist, saying that I had come there to bring them the Word of God, and that he ought not to be begging of me. I was touched by the evidence of sincerity in their attention, drawn forth by this solitary beggar; and I went on to show them their need of the bread of life. Then I told them of the impossibility of finding that bread under the system of Romanism to which they were bound, strongly pointing out the necessity for deciding to belong to Christ, and to leave the Mass.

I would not allow myself to judge of the effect at the time; but rather storing up the recollections of the feeling shown by the people, to enable me the better to judge of the reports I might hereafter receive from those who might carry on the work, I left them with a blessing. The two priests who had been receiving confessions at the next house came out shortly after I had set forward on my walk to Oughterard, with the Reader and the Schoolmaster, accompanied by several persons from the cabin. They mounted their horses and cantered by us, but relaxing their pace, they enabled us to overtake them again. I walked by their side for some distance, to afford them an opportunity of speaking to me if they wished; but they said nothing, and we outstripped them by walking fast to the town.

In the subsequent passages of the Story of

the Irish Church Missions, it will soon be perceived how important a part this little Mission of Castelkerke (originally but an episode) was destined to bear in the general current of events which led to the organization of the Society for Irish Church Missions; and even by itself this episode cannot be without a lively interest, from the nature of the singular incidents which rendered it such an illustration of the great truth, that "the hairs of our head are all numbered."

CHAPTER X.

In the gradual progress of events which led to the formation of the Society for Irish Church Missions, there were two circumstances which turned out to be of essential importance, and which may properly be related at the point of the story at which we have arrived. Though different in character, they combined to give a strong impulse to the Missionary work. These shall be placed before the reader.

It has been already stated that there was no intention of forming any organized machinery for the work of Missions, until such an arrangement may be said to have been forced upon the promoters of the object. The earnest desire of Mr. Durant and myself was to arouse the Irish Clergy to an active aggression upon Roman principles, under the circumstances of preparation in the hearts of the people of which we were so fully convinced;

and to lead them to enlarge the operations of the Irish Society, and other instrumentalities, so as to suit them to the requirements of the times. We had no other object than this.

The Christian men with whom I had intercourse at that time could not partake of our view, and therefore were not stirred in the direction we so anxiously desired; but, on the contrary, manifested the opinion that our movement was neither judicious nor safe. We had many conversations on the subject, in which were discussed the means that might be used to convince their judgment, and excite them to the necessary course. From these conversations it resulted that, in order to convince our cautious brethren, nothing would be more useful than to exhibit to them the fruits of an experimental Mission, carried on upon the principles which had been proposed to them, and which we believed to be suited to the occasion.

In the retrospect of memory, the conversation with Mr. Durant in which this point was decided often rises prominently to my mind, with all its surrounding circumstances, and all the power of feeling which was drawn forth. "How can we have such an experimental Mission? Who would undertake it?" I quoted the words of the prophet, "Here am I; send me." The expense might, perhaps, be considerable, but Mr. Durant said he would willingly meet that. The question arose, to what point such a Mission should be directed? The Blue Book of the Census of 1841 was at hand, and he laid it upon the table. I was about to open it, when he said, "Stop! Let us pray for direction." With my hand still upon the volume we knelt down, and I very earnestly implored that the Holy Spirit Himself might point out the direction in which we were to move, and give wisdom and grace in every step we took; that it might all be to the glory of Jesus Christ in the salvation of Irish Roman Catholic souls. Mr. Durant's fervent and expressive "Amen!" testified to the certainty that we might claim the precious promise—"If two of you shall agree on earth as touching anything that they shall ask, it shall be done for them of my Father which is in heaven."

Mr. Durant opened the Blue Book at the end, where are found the various maps which are given to express to the eye the results of the details of the Census. He turned to the map of education, where the light tinge which distinguishes Ulster gradually becomes dark, until it grows into deep black in the west and south-west of the island. "To make the experiment effective," said he, "the Mission should be carried on where the ignorance is greatest, and the advantages are fewest. The difficulties will, of course, be greater; but the success would be more telling, and more likely to convince the Irish Clergy." He put his finger on a deep black spot in the map, and said, "Where is that?" This was the west of Galway. We referred to the figures of the Census, and found that the proportion of those who could read, compared with the population, was distressingly small. Subsequent examination of statistics showed that this was indeed a land of darkness. There existed only two churches in a journey of sixty miles. Three clergymen ministered in the Church of England in a breadth of land which contained 40,000 souls; and even the Roman Catholic ministrations were few and far between; so that whole tracts of country were left to the barbarism of superstitions masked with the name of a false Christianity. Surely there are few heathen districts that stood so greatly in need of the light carried by a Christian missionary.

I gladly accepted what I considered a call to undertake this missionary adventure. It was settled that I should select three or four of my Messenger Agents to accompany me, as the Lord might guide me, through this black country of the map; and that, while I preached Christ's salvation, and openly contrasted it with the deceitful salvation proposed through the Mass, I should make use of these agents in gathering the people, and diffusing amongst them the knowledge of the true gospel.

In bringing my readers to this point, I feel strongly tempted to picture to them in detail some of the many striking incidents which occurred in my first missionary efforts at Galway, and the immediate neighbourhood of Oughterard. But it would extend this story in an unreasonable and unhistorical degree, if I were to yield to this temptation. Almost every incident possessed a peculiar interest, to create which in the reader would require peculiar picturing; and I must, therefore, be satisfied with generalizing the result.

Every step that was taken gave a fresh testimony to the correctness of the judgment that had been formed of the prepared state of the people. In the midst of great ignorance and habitual slavish submission to the priests, there was an evident desire to listen to the instruction that was offered to them. Frequent demonstrations of threatened violence were but the mask which covered the real desire of their hearts. This was the effect of their slavery. On the other hand, their real desire was manifested in the cautious night-gatherings here and there, to listen to the teaching against which they shouted and threatened in the daylight. It was seen in the private inquiries made by many, and the manner in which they listened while they seemed to be deaf, and received, while they seemed to reject, the Agents' visits.

The difficulties were greater in the town of Galway itself than in the surrounding country. The population of the borough was 22,000, and the Protestants amongst them numbered little more than 1000, with one church in which to worship. Four nunneries and two or three monasteries characterized the place as being perhaps the most Popish in Ireland; while the antique appearance of the houses in one part, which was originally a Spanish settlement, added to this character that of seeming a foreign town. We found many impediments in executing our Mission here, and were sometimes threatened with apparent danger, which, however, was averted by a bold and calm disregard of threats. Of the four Agents I took with me, three showed themselves equal to this in several emergencies, but the fourth too plainly showed that he had not courage. Alas! he has since shown that he had not faith. He was a young convert who had been turned out of the house by his father, and of whom I had formed a favourable opinion, though not a decided one. He had acquired the phraseology of a spiritual man, without having the life of the Spirit; and some years afterwards he was overcome by great temptations, he married a Papist, and relapsed into Popery. He is one of the very few instances in which a some time trusted convert has disappointed our expectations. Even now I have a lingering hope that, through fire, this poor fellow will be brought to the foot of the Cross.

It may be well to give one instance of the nature of this struggle in Galway; which, perhaps, can best be done by relating an occurrence which took place some time after our first efforts there, but which will show the effect they produced.

I had made friendly acquaintance with the clergy in Galway, who were all right-minded

Christian men. The late Warden was eminent both as a preacher and a Christian. He was also a controversialist, and had not neglected to attend to the state of the Roman Catholics about him, having in years gone by encouraged controversial sermons in his church, and preached several himself. The result, however, had been far from encouraging, and had left the impression that it was useless to make such efforts. This impression had unhappily been stereotyped upon the minds of the clergy, and remained there fresh after many years and many changes. The collegiate church of St. Nicholas, Galway, had then a corporation consisting of a Warden and four Vicars. These four were responsible for the duties of the church week by week. I asked to be permitted to preach a controversial sermon in the church. This was courteously declined, and I was told that such an act, as beginning a controversy, would be sure to produce very distressing differences, and perhaps dangerous consequences, without any adequate result. My arguments had no effect upon these good men. It was the beginning of controversy that they dreaded. Of course they would be ready to meet any Roman Catholic who flung down the gauntlet to them, and they would expect the same from the whole array of priests in Galway if they began an open attack on their faith. They showed every kindness, but no concession to my wishes.

Some time afterwards I was journeying to the West, and meant only to sleep in Galway, on my way to Castelkerke. I arrived there on a Monday afternoon; and as the coach drove into the town, I found the walls placarded with great bills, announcing that the new organ in the chapel of the Augustinian convent was to be opened on the previous Sunday. A choir and celebrated singers were advertised by name; and it was stated in large characters that the celebrated Dr. Cahill would preach a sermon on the infallibility of the Church of Rome.

Here was controversy commenced, and the gauntlet thrown down. I found on inquiry that the chapel had been crowded to excess, and a large number of the Protestants had been present. I lost no time in calling on the Vicar who had charge of the church for the following week, and I pointed out how the gauntlet had been thrown down, and that of course he would not allow his Protestant congregation to be led astray by Dr. Cahill.

Unless he intended to take up that gauntlet himself, I was ready to do so next Sunday.

Though he could not deny the force of my argument, he was reluctant to act upon it, and pleaded that he could not take such a step without the consent of the Warden; if he agreed, I might preach in answer to Dr. Cahill. I forthwith paid a visit to the Warden, who evinced the same feeling as the Vicar, but said that if the latter consented, he would not object to my preaching. Thus the matter was settled, and I did not leave the town until I had got a placard printed as large as Dr. Cahill's, announcing that a sermon would be preached on the following Sunday evening in St. Nicholas Church, to meet the teaching of last Sunday on the infallibility of the Church of Rome.

I returned to Galway on the Saturday, and found that great excitement prevailed in the town. The good-natured chambermaid at the hotel besought me with tears not to risk my life, as I was sure to be killed if I preached the sermon. I called on the Vicar, who told me that, though it was too late to draw back, he was alarmed at the excitement which prevailed, and that not a few of the Protestants had expressed their apprehensions and their disapprobation. I asked to be allowed to preach to the Protestant congregation at the morning service, which was readily granted.

On Sunday morning my sermon contained a simple explanation of the duty of Protestant Christians living amongst Roman Catholics, as resulting from their great privileges in the gospel themselves, which I plainly set forth. The evening came. The way from the hotel in the great square is down a long street called Shop Street, towards the end of which a narrow lane leads to St. Nicholas Church. This stands at the end of a large graveyard, which is surrounded by high iron rails. There were evident marks of malice in the countenances of the people who were gathering in groups in the street, and as my person was known, these were unmistakably directed upon me. On arriving at the church, there were very few persons in it. The prayers began, and but few were added to the number. Towards the end of the prayers, however, the church began to fill. The previous occupants of the pews were plainly Protestants, and the new comers were as plainly Romanists. The church is cruciform. The pulpit and desk stand in the centre of the cross, closing the east portion away from the congregation to form a chapter-house. The Communion-table and rails stand immediately under the pulpit. The organ is placed at the end of the length of the cross, where there is an entrance. The two arms or transepts are broad, the main door is at the end of the northern transept, while there is no door in the southern. This description is necessary, that the reader may understand what occurred.

When the first Romanists began to enter the church they were followed rapidly by others, as a flock of sheep will go after the few that first break through a hedge. They filled all the vacant seats in the church and the northern transept. Very few went round the rails to get into the southern; but before the hymn was over every seat was occupied, and the broad aisles were crammed with those who stood. The habit of superstitious reverence for an altar restrained the crowd from passing the table, so that the space on the left of the preacher was comparatively empty.

After earnest prayer, both audibly and internally, I began my sermon, and this produced a storm of shouts and yells. I thank God that I felt thoroughly self-possessed in reliance upon the Holy Spirit, whose help I earnestly asked, while the discordant yells were going on. They ceased, and I began again to preach; they began again to shout. I folded my arms, and manifested a calm determination which at last overcame them, and won them to silence. When I had a hearing, I divided my subject into four heads, and continued to preach uninterruptedly for three-quarters of an hour by my watch, which was lying by my side. This had exhausted three of the heads I had marked out; and, just as I was about to begin the fourth, a child in one of the pews, who had dropped asleep, fell from the bench and gave a loud cry. There was a sort of ante-chapel at the northern door, in which some men, whom we should call "roughs," were standing. At the disturbance caused by the child's cry these men uttered loud shouts; and rushing upon the body of people who were standing closely packed in the northern aisle, pushed them forward with an impulse which affected the whole crowd, and made the foremost rush past the communion rails into the southern transept, uttering screams of terror rather than shouts of disturbance. The alarm communicated itself to the whole congregation; the whistles and shouts which proceeded from the men at the north door kept up the panic. The banging of pew doors, as persons strove to get out and others strove to pass them, sounded like a desultory fire of musketry; and the climax was added to this intense confusion when, over and above the storm of screams and shouts, the voice of a sergeant-major, who had ten or a dozen soldiers with him (and who, according to the orders at that time, brought with them their arms when they attended any public place) issued the word of command, "Fix bayonets!" followed by the rattle of steel.

I do not remember ever to have been in a more distressing position. A thousand thoughts were rushing through my mind; the state of the people; the difficulty of appeasing them; the consequences to the cause I had in hand. The Warden and two of the Vicars were sitting in the desk; would they feel justified in prohibiting future efforts? But the sergeant's word of command brought these thoughts to a practical point. If his voice were audible above the noise, so might mine be. I ventured on prayer, not in the less than whisper which reaches the ear of Him to whom it is addressed, but in a sound that might make the people know that I prayed.

In a voice as loud as the word of command, I said, "O God, calm the people, take away fear, give thy Holy Spirit;" and then, as a word of command, I cried out, "Take your seats!"

Never was prayer more signally or distinctly answered. The people did take their seats, and that, too, at once. It scarcely required a couple of minutes to find them arranged in decent order. Two women were taken out fainting, and the rest settled themselves in pews; and, though fewer in number, it was even then a full congregation. I briefly returned thanks to God, and then proceeded with the fourth head of my subject, which occupied twenty minutes by the watch at my side. With a prayer and a blessing I dismissed the congregation, who separated with respectable quietness.

When I went down to the chapter-room, the Warden and the Vicars shook hands with me, and thanked God as they offered me the use of the pulpit on future occasions. Presently people came in, warning me not to go out into the streets, or I should surely be pulled to pieces, the crowd was so immense and exasperated. A police sergeant came to assure me that he would protect me, as he had twenty men with him at the gate. I told him that I did not send for him, and asked him who did. He said that one of the magistrates who was in the congregation had sent for him and given him orders. I thanked him and the magistrate, but requested that he would testify that I had not sent for him. My knowledge of human nature convinced me that a display of fear is the sure way to produce insult; and I knew the Irish well enough to feel that a manifestation of bold confidence is sure to avert danger. I left the church accompanied by the Vicars, and, when we came outside the rails of the churchyard, the riot was indeed tremendous. "Here he comes!" "The devil himself!" "He is black in the face!" "Luther!" etc., etc., etc. These were mild compared to the curses, which, I am sorry to say, sounded mostly from female voices. There were some policemen drawn up in line in front of the gate. I told the sergeant he had better disperse them amongst the crowd, which would be better protection than an escort, and not so aggravating to the people. We turned up Shop Street, and, if I had not determined to walk on, with the risk of treading on the toes of the women who danced backward in front of me with the most insulting exclamations, we should never have got on at all. But we did get on, and arrived at a nook in the street, the entrance of a small blind alley. When we came in front of this, there issued forth a continuous shower of large stones; these had the effect of ridding me of my besetting women, constant relays of whom had danced before me hitherto, and only one stone struck my hat, though my companion received rather a severe blow on the shoulder. This stoning, however, was very near the end of the street; and when we got into the square, and arrived at the door of the hotel, the master, himself a Romanist, was anxiously trying to pull me up the two or three steps in front to get me out of danger. I thanked him, but walked up the steps, and, standing upon the highest, I looked over an immense crowd, probably more than 1000 people, most of them shouting and yelling. I remembered the lesson I had learnt from the sergeant in the church, and raising my voice like an adjutant manœuvring a thousand men, I cried out, "Stop!" There was an instant silence, while I added, in the same voice, "Thank you, my friends, for taking care of me safely home. Good night." There was a universal burst of laughter, and I entered the hotel with these cheerful sounds in my ears.

During the difficult progress from the door of the church to the steps of the hotel, I had not failed to speak some words of peace from time to time to those near me, especially when we first issued forth from the iron gates of the churchyard, and when we had to pause in the outburst of the storm I have described. It never occurred to me that these words for Christ could even have been heard, as they were uttered out of the deep compassion I felt for the people. Eighteen years afterwards, a woman died in a hospital, and being a long time a convert, one of the missionaries attended her in her last illness. She told him that she had been a bigoted Romanist in Galway, and was present in that crowd in Shop Street. She then heard one of those words for Christ which were spoken out of that compassion, and, observing the calmness with which these insults were borne, it fastened the word on her mind, and the Holy Spirit fastened it in her heart, and to that beginning she traced her conversion and her salvation.

I have given these circumstances in detail, because they may serve as a fair specimen of the manner in which we had to get through the surf, before we could launch the vessel of the Irish Church Missions, and bring her into deep water: and the reader will immediately perceive that if such a specimen were to be given at all, it must be in its full detail, as there can be no possibility of condensing the account of such events into a few sentences, so as to communicate a specimen of the manner and difficulties of the work. But while this specimen shows the difficulties of the surf, we can now speak of the effect produced by working through it perseveringly. A regular Mission was afterwards established in Galway. It would be anticipatory to speak of that at present; it will be enough to state, that eight years afterwards I went to Galway to meet in a Church Mission schoolroom 93 adult converts and 105 children, for the most part children of Romanists, who willingly allowed them to attend a Mission school. These and other results of the blessing of God in the Mission work must be reserved for their proper place in the story.

Having thus explained the first of the two important events to which I alluded in the beginning, I will reserve the account of the second for the next chapter.

CHAPTER XI.

At the beginning of the foregoing chapter it was stated that two circumstances were of essential importance to the progress of the work, and that they might properly be related at the point of the story at which we have arrived. The opening of the experimental Mission in the West was one of these, and has been laid before the reader in that chapter. The other was the culminating point of all the preparatory efforts in the West, in engaging the interest and influence of the Bishop of Tuam in the work. It would be impossible to convey a correct idea of the working of Providence in bringing about this important event, without going back to a much earlier period, the story of which may be said to develop more strikingly the designs and minute operations of Providence, than any other portion of the history.

I have shown in the beginning, how God began afar off, in the year 1840, an early preparation for carrying out his purposes, by moving the most unlikely instrument that men could have chosen for work among the Irish. For a long time I thought that this was the first of the hairs that was numbered for such a use, but I afterwards found that it was but part of the divine plan which He had begun to set in motion years before. He opened the spring of a rivulet of prayer in the same mountains which He designed for the first fields of the work, and it flowed on and on until its effect was to be found in calling forth the unsuitable instrumentality five hundred miles off.

There is a neat little town in Connemara called Clifden. It was built early in the present century by John D'Arcy, Esq., the representative of an ancient and honourable family, and the possessor of large tracts of land in those lovely mountains. For the pleasure and benefit of the sea, he was accustomed to leave his house at the eastern part of the county; and at last he built a large house which he called Clifden Castle, and then the town, to which he invited tradespeople and artisans. In the course of twenty years, a population of 1200 inhabited this settlement, which thus centralized the scattered population of nearly 50,000 souls spread over the district from the Killeries on the North to the Bay of Galway on the South.

Mr. D'Arcy had a large family. His eldest son Hyacinth received his early education at the excellent institution of Vanheigel, in Dublin; thence he went to Trinity College. After two years at college, the affliction of a painful disease of the knee-joint made his removal necessary. After trials of various places and remedies, Mr. H. D'Arcy suffered so much from almost every motion on land, that he lived mainly on a little yacht, with which he delighted to thread the mazes of the many inlets of the sea which indent that coast, and gave it the name of Connemara, or the Bays of the Sea.

It was in the relief from pain, and enjoyment of the sea, which thus filled up his time, that light began dimly to dawn on his mind. It was a long dawning before the Sun of righteousness broke through the early clouds and shone in brightness on his soul. Gradually the truth grew upon him; but in the year 1827 he was so far advanced in Christian decision that he then made an entry in his diary that he devoted himself unreservedly to God. By a happy coincidence his second brother James, and a sister, were led very much in the same way to the same point. The rector of the parish was the Rev. A. Thomas, the same person who, in so persevering a manner, induced me to go to Ireland, as described in the second chapter. He was a sincere Christian, and what he preached was the truth of the gospel, so that amongst the small congregation of Protestants in Clifden the D'Arcys were nourished with the bread of life.

Archbishop Trench (the last Protestant Archbishop of Tuam) had given permission to Mr. Thomas to undertake the management of the Irish branch of the Society for Promoting Christianity among the Jews, and a very respectable man, the Rev. Mark Antony Foster, who knew the truth, took his place as his curate for the service of the Protestants of Clifden, with whom matters went on very quietly, except that Mr. D'Arcy was not a little disturbed at the growing religious tendencies of his sons. The Archbishop, considering the immense extent of the great union of Ballinakill, associated another curate with Mr. Foster in this great charge, and generously paid himself the stipends of both. The Rev. Brabazon Ellis, this co-curate, lived principally at Roundstone. He was a man of a lively and earnest spirit, who could not rest satisfied in the darkness around him, and began to make an aggressive movement upon Romanism. Hyacinth and James D'Arcy heartily joined in the movement; Mr. Foster quietly consented; and Colonel Thompson, who was the possessor of an estate at Salruck, some eighteen miles beyond Clifden, added his name, and these formed a Committee for the purpose of gathering the means for establishing a settlement at Salruck, with the direct object of the conversion of the Romanists.

The first step taken by this Committee was to issue an appeal for funds in the form of a placard. The nature of this appeal will be sufficiently gathered from the striking words with which it was headed :—"Forty thousand souls lying in darkness and the shadow of death!" The effect produced by the circulation of this paper will be readily conceived. It manifested an abundance of zeal, which, however, needed the painful training of experience. While the excitement was great it was accompanied by the concurrence of some friends who were able to give assistance.

Money was collected, plans were formed, and some buildings, at small cost, were erected at Salruck.

But the effort was too sudden, and, perhaps, too violent, for the state of things. The priests fulminated curses; special preachers were sent from Galway to alarm and excite the people; the sermon of one of these was taken down and appeared in a local paper. He told the people "that the Bible was poison, and advised them to drive out with violence any person who would bring them such a destructive book," and he concluded his sermon by saying, "that every Protestant in existence has the brand of the devil on his forehead." The Christian Committee were not armed with a sufficiently-sustained power for continuance against all the difficulties which stood in their way. Some of the plans were found impracticable, and after a while the excitement subsided. The appeal was issued in 1835, and before the end of 1836 it had apparently died away.

But there was life left in the ashes of this effort. A few, a very few Romanists had received the truth, and managed through all the extreme difficulty of their circumstances to cleave to that salvation which had been brought to them by God's grace in this passing flash of life. A rich fruit resulted in the fact, that Hyacinth and James D'Arcy then laid hold of a hope that there was a blessing in store for Connemara, which was to be sought by earnest prayer. They determined to gather regularly once a week the little band that had been influenced, with some Christian Protestants of the congregation, and to pass some time in prayer for the special object that God would send the light of his truth to the people of Connemara. It was no easy matter to arrange for such a prayer-meeting under such circumstances; but from the year 1836, Mr. D'Arcy assures me that he does not recollect a single week up to the present time on which this prayer-meeting was ever given up. Seven o'clock on Friday evening was sure to find one or both of the brothers at the appointed place. When the company at the Castle rendered it difficult for both to be absent, one or the other slipped from the dinner-table with as little observation as might be. The gatherings were very small, but the D'Arcys were not discouraged; sometimes but one could join them, or two, or three, or four; but they had always enough to plead the Lord's promise, " Where two or three are gathered in my name, there am I," and confident in their Lord's presence, they ceased not to plead earnestly, and give Him no rest until He should establish and make Connemara a praise in the earth.

Here is to be found the earliest source of the blessings vouchsafed through the Irish Church Missions. God planted the seed of the blessing by laying the matter upon the heart of these Christian men. The turning up of the earth, so to speak, for this planting made disturbance in which the hidden seed was laid safely, watered by prayer, covered and secured in patience. They waited for twelve or thirteen years before there was a sign of an answer. While grace was working in Connemara, Providence began in 1840 to work at Wonston, and it was not till 1847 that these two branches of the work became openly united. How many hairs were numbered for this work until they became plaited together in the chain of God's wonders.

In the year 1837 it was considered necessary that Mr. Hyacinth D'Arcy's leg should be amputated, by which his capacity of motion was greatly increased, as he was relieved from the suffering to which he had been so many years accustomed. Two years afterwards his father died. Mr. John D'Arcy had lived like so many of the higher class of Irish landed proprietors, without reference to the limit of their incomes. Mortgages on land were easily obtained, and constantly resorted to. The result, as a general rule, has been testified by the establishment of the Encumbered Estates Court. Mr. D'Arcy was no exception to this rule, and he left his son an honoured name, a pleasant castle, and an estate on which the mortgages and claims greatly exceeded its saleable value. But Hyacinth D'Arcy was a man of God, and, surrounded by intense difficulties, he knew how to confide in the promises of God to his people; and those promises have been fulfilled to him in a large extension of subsequent important usefulness.

It was in the year 1845 that the two ladies who were such helps in the early work visited Clifden, in the course of a tour to inquire into the state of the people. Here they became acquainted with Mr. D'Arcy, and were enabled to appreciate his Christian anxiety for the benefit of the Romish population. United in the same great object, they joined in their efforts to attain it. Early in September, 1847, a letter from Miss Bellingham to Mr. D'Arcy contained the following passage:—"A very great friend of Ireland is to be in Dublin next week—Mr. Dallas, of Wonston—only for three days. I am sure he would like to hear your account of Connemara. He has done so much for Captain Blake's locality, I should like much to interest him for Clifden. Might I ask him to call upon you?" Mr. D'Arcy came up to Dublin and we met. Then was the confluence of the two streams of prayer for Ireland, the springs of which had begun to flow so many years before—one in the mountains of Connemara, the other in the downs of Hampshire—and which have flowed on ever since; while many hearts have been added to deepen and widen the stream on which the Lord has sent the gospel, not to Connemara only, but to so many thirsty spots in the spiritual desert of Ireland. The intercourse with Mr. Hyacinth D'Arcy led to knowledge, plans, and arrangements, which greatly advanced the progress of the work, and opened the way to much practical development of the great object in view.

The form which the operations had already assumed made me perceive the great importance of losing no time in anticipating many difficulties, by giving to the movement a proper ecclesiastical character; and the plans which grew out of my intercourse with Mr. D'Arcy confirmed me in the necessity for establishing a principle of order in the work. The difficulty was how to accomplish this object. The visit to Ireland in September, 1847, when I first met Mr. D'Arcy, took me to Castelkerke. Matters were progressing there very rapidly; an intelligent and clever agent, a convert, who had been educated at Maynooth for the Roman priesthood, was acting there very diligently as a Scripture-Reader. On the Sunday I spent at Castelkerke, I preached to a crowded congregation of attentive hearers; some already converts, and others sufficiently loosened from Rome to dare the denunciations of the priests specially directed against the Castelkerke teaching. The Sunday-school in the afternoon so filled the room that the smaller children were placed outside. In closing my sermon I asked them whether they thought they would continue steadfast as a Christian congregation, if a minister were settled amongst them; and the response I received was unhesitating and unanimous.

On the evening of the next day, a few friends were consulting on the matter after dinner, at Doone House. The Rev. Mr.

Moore, the Rector of Cong, was with us. I stated that the proper step to be taken would be to have a regular ministry of a missionary character settled at Castelkerke. All present agreed to the propriety of this, but who was to be the minister? A clergyman of the Church was out of the question, for he must speak Irish; perhaps a Wesleyan minister, or a Presbyterian, of both which denominations there were settlements in Galway. I stated distinctly that the minister must be a clergyman of the Church of England, or I could have nothing to do with the movement; and that the best way would be to ask the Bishop of the diocese, in such an exceptional case, to ordain a suitable man for the purpose. Every one present declared that the thing was impossible, though the rector coincided in my view of the subject. There was much discussion, which closed by my stating that the work was of God, and that to secure his blessing we must take the right course with whatever difficulties it might seem to be surrounded; and that we could leave the result to the ordering of his Providence. To settle the matter at once, I determined to go to Tuam the next day, and to lay the whole matter personally before the Bishop. The remonstrances of our lay friends were of no avail, and Mr. Moore very willingly agreed to accompany me, though he confessed that it was with little expectation of a successful result.

In the dark dawn of a September morning, on which a leaden canopy of cloud greatly retarded the light, a car was at the door, and we mounted the seats amidst a downpour of rain, the straight descent of which gave us no hope of any favourable change. Our host at parting urged this impossible weather as a token to enforce his remonstrances. I had engaged to go to Dublin by the mail that night, and instead of joining it at Galway, I intended to meet it at three o'clock at Tuam; but we had thirty-six Irish miles to travel in the rain with the same horse in order to reach Tuam, and the prospect was not cheering. Only that the Providential angels had orders in the matter, and that particular hairs were numbered for the occasion, there would have been abundant reasons for relinquishing the journey; and but for divine grace, a fainting heart would have acted upon these sufficient reasons. The rain damped the desire for conversation, and I had time for much secret prayer in the seven hours which elapsed before we saw the tall tower of St. Jarlath's. I was wet through to the skin, as I told the driver, on entering Tuam, when he replied with characteristic humour, "Only to the skin, sir—sure I'm wet through to the bone!"

It was one o'clock; if anything was to be done, it must be before three. So—wet as we were—we drove straight to the palace. The Bishop received us in his study. Mr. Moore introduced me by name, and I thought it best then to introduce myself more particularly, by stating my position in the Church, my independence of Irish expectations, etc., etc., which led to a brief statement of the singular course of events that had made me interested in Ireland. I told him my aggression on Rome at Castelkerke, and the interesting results, the details of which Mr. Moore confirmed. I suggested the great importance of adopting the movement into the Church, and the danger that might result from any other course, and mentioned this as my motive for intruding upon his lordship.

The Bishop listened with attention, and showed his interest by various questions. He said he had already heard something of the state of things at Castelkerke, and asked what I wished him to do. I told him that we would find the means of supporting a missionary clergyman for that district, if he would sanction the movement, and license a suitable minister who could speak the Irish language, and was able to live amongst the people, and could conform to their habits and the difficulties of the position. The Bishop asked where such a man could be found. I answered that I knew of such a one whom I could recommend, if his lordship would consent, under all the circumstances, to dispense with the usual conventional qualifications, and being satisfied as to piety and knowledge, would ordain a person for the purpose.

The Bishop's interest evidently increased in the course of the conversation; and after many questions concerning the individual in question, he said that he would consider the matter, and would make further inquiries himself, and then write to me. There was something in his manner which begat a hopeful feeling; and the difficulty I found in rising from my chair, to which my saturated clothes adhered, made him laugh heartily. He has often referred to this visit of the "drowned rats" in our subsequent intimate intercourse.

The Bishop acted upon his expressed intention—he sent two clergymen to make special inquiries in the locality mentioned.

Their report confirmed the statement we had made. I paid him another visit at Tuam in November, and after full consideration he consented to confer deacon's orders on Mr. John O'Callaghan. Our correspondence in the course of the business had led to a nearer acquaintance; and in January, 1848, on the day of the ordination in the cathedral at Tuam, the Bishop invited me to the palace, and desired me to preach the sermon upon the occasion. This was a turning point in the history of the movement. It settled its ecclesiastical character. It engaged the Bishop of that vast diocese in its operations; and it began an intercourse between his lordship and myself, which deepened in interest and ripened in affection until the day of his lamented death, eighteen years afterwards.

CHAPTER XII.

The Irish famine of 1847 had touched the hearts of the British public, and a very large amount had been placed in the hands of a Committee of gentlemen in London, which was called the British Association for the relief of that famine. Among other plans, a sum of £100,000 was devoted to the supply of a daily ration of food to the children in the schools, of all denominations. When Mr. D'Arcy came up to Dublin, in September, 1847, one of his objects was to arrange that the bounty of this Association should be fairly extended to the district of Connemara. In the rules for applying this grant, the bounty was limited to a supply for the schools already in existence. The rumour of this plan had gone before its actual organization, and the Roman priests had collected together in their chapels all the children in each district. The

Poor Law Inspector (it was through this agency that the arrangement was to be carried out) told me, that on his first visit he found the chapels crowded with children without a book, or a slate, or anything which could give the gathering the character of a school.

The Protestant gentlemen of Connemara acted upon the early information, but with more honesty and effect. There was at Clifden a Protestant parochial school, where there were from twelve to fourteen boys. The Christian Committee spoken of in the last chapter had left about £100 in the hands of the Treasurer. It had often been a question how this was to be employed, and now it became available for the purpose of getting up some schools in the surrounding district. There was an old National School-house at Sellerna, neglected and dilapidated, which was now occupied, and a pensioner, who lived in the neighbourhood, was engaged to collect the children, and to act as schoolmaster. A cabin was engaged at Ballyconree, and one of the senior boys at Clifden was sent to keep school there; while at Errislanon a few pounds were expended in raising a poor building, where another boy from the Clifden School was sent on the same errand. These schools were actually in operation when Mr. D'Arcy came to Dublin to confer with Count Stralyckie, a Polish nobleman, under whose management this department was placed.

While in the Romish Chapel-Schools, so-called, there was literally no instruction at all, in these Protestant Schools the Scriptures were made a main part of the instruction given; and their being so, happily presented no barrier to the ready attendance of the children, so that a goodly number were found in each of these Schools, and the great object of the Christian people who had commenced them was to find the means by which they could be supported and continued. I arranged with Mr. D'Arcy to pay a visit to Clifden as soon as I possibly could, and fulfilled my promise at the end of the year 1847.

It may be truly said, "The famine was sore in the land." It is an appalling thing to pass through a population of starving people. As I walked up one of the streets in Galway, there was a tall girl some distance before me. I observed that she staggered, and I quickened my pace to help her; but before I reached her she fell, and I found scarcely more than a human skeleton wrapped in a single garment, and apparently expiring; and in the course of a quarter of an hour she did expire. Those who removed the body seemed to take small note of the event, a token of the general condition of the people.

My visit to Clifden was one of great importance and deep interest. Mr. D'Arcy received me at the Castle with warm, brotherly affection. We consulted prayerfully concerning the steps to be taken; and in my future visits, which from thenceforth became frequent, the progressive steps in the Missionary work became more and more evident and encouraging. I must not occupy these pages with the full detail of each visit; but it will be enough if I state some of the more striking events which occurred on the several occasions.

We went out to see the school at Ballyconree. It was held in a cabin at the gate of the approach to the Glebe House, which was a poor building very much out of order. The drive over the mountain from Clifden Castle is one of the wildest in the West of Ireland. When you have climbed, as it were, to the crest of the mountain by very steep roads, the Atlantic bursts upon you, dotted with numerous islands, and the line of the coast broken by slender promontories. Leaving the Bay of Clifden, you descend upon Streamstown Bay, the mountain dividing the two. Numerous cabins are scattered between the rocks, almost all of the meaner sort; and, passing through them by a narrow road, you are brought to the gate of the Glebe "Avenue," as every approach to a house is called, though unmarked by a single tree.

At the door of the cabin where the school was kept there was a gathering of persons of all ages, each bearing the mark of the famine in their appearance. We entered, and most of them went in with us, crowding up the children who formed the school. I addressed them in simple language; spoke to them of the value of their souls; told them of the salvation of Christ, and of the blessed truths contained in the Holy Scriptures; then urged that the teaching of Rome was not in the Scriptures, and that the value of the school consisted in the teaching of God's Word to their children and to themselves. The people listened with attention, and showed marks of pleasure sufficient to encourage us; and I closed my address by promising that further instruction should be given them in that cabin, and that if the people sent their children and came themselves in such numbers as would press out its walls, we would take measures to build them a larger and a better school-house in which to meet. I am happy to say that, by the blessing of God, both the condition and the promise were afterwards fulfilled.

In consultation with Mr. D'Arcy as to the future steps to be taken, it was settled that a Mission should be undertaken in a large and populous promontory lying between the Bays of Streamstown and Cleggan, called Sellerna. The people were chiefly fishermen, all Roman Catholics except a few coastguards. The distance from Clifden was about eight miles, and the priests of Clifden seldom took the trouble of the journey, so that the population were greatly neglected in every way. A plan was arranged for a spiritual invasion of this neglected land of darkness, and it was put into execution without delay. I was acquainted with a valued and Christian young student, who has since become a diligent and useful clergyman. I sent for him to come to me in England. He was acquainted with the Irish language from his earliest years, and was therefore suited to the work we had in view at Sellerna. Upon our Lord's principle of sending out labourers two together, and to balance the youthfulness of the Irishman, I selected an excellent man of Christian experience in England; and, bringing them together, I gave them distinct instructions and a solemn charge. I warned them of the difficulties, and pointed them to the Power which would enable them to overcome all difficulties, and pass through all dangers. I explained to them, also, the sources of encouragement which led us on. I went with them to London; and having commended them to God in earnest prayer, I saw them off with a hopeful heart.

This was in the very early days of January, 1848. They went to their work boldly, and very soon produced an excitement in Sellerna. Much discussion took place. A man of some standing in the place admitted them to his cottage, which became a scene of controversy without violence, though with occasional outbursts of characteristic warmth. It happened, however, that the winter weather became unusually severe. Much snow fell, and remained on the ground, which is rare on that coast. Our earnest Missionaries went on with their work in spite of this serious hindrance in their journeys to Sellerna. This, however, was suddenly stopped by the illness of the elder, who was unequal to sustain the hardships they had to encounter. He was seized with paralysis, and with difficulty reached his home. He has since died, and I fear he never recovered the effects of that winter campaign in the Lord's service.

An experienced Scripture-Reader was shortly afterwards sent to carry on the good work which had been begun in Sellerna. He produced a considerable stir in the place, and roused the opposition of the Clifden priests, who went out there and anathematized all who should attend to the teaching of the Reader. In spite of this, the discussions at the house of Patrick Joyce, where they had begun, continued to be frequented, and Patrick himself studied the Douay Bible in order to confute the heretic. On one occasion the Reader had explained the fourth chapter of the Acts, and showed the early opposition to the gospel, even as it was at that very day; and he closed with the twelfth verse, setting forth Jesus Christ as the only but the complete salvation. After a long discussion on this, the Reader set forth to return to Clifden. Not long after, the priest, accompanied by two farmers, all on horseback, came to Joyce's house to seek for the Reader; and, being informed that he had returned to Clifden on foot, they went in pursuit of him. He was overtaken in a lonely part of the road, and the two farmers set on the poor fellow with their shilalahs, and gave him a severe beating, while the priest sat on his horse to witness the castigation.

When the Reader reported at Clifden what had occurred, Mr. D'Arcy went out to Sellerna, and he found Patrick Joyce, with several others, greatly excited, and struck by the coincidence of the Reader's teaching from Acts iv., and the illustration of it in the priest's conduct. "Sure, sir, it's the fourth chapter of Acts over again," they exclaimed; and the subsequent conversion of Patrick Joyce himself, and of others who were there, may be traced, under God's blessing, to this coincidence.

I was at Castelkerke at the time this happened, and I immediately went to Clifden. We sent out a Reader to Sellerna to remain there, and to invite the people from house to house to send all their children to meet me on the following Thursday, at an old ruined building which had formerly been a storehouse, but was now deserted. It consisted of two floors, with a ladder by which to reach the upper. At the time appointed, Mr. D'Arcy and myself, with some friends, drove out to Sellerna. As we approached the building, we perceived many people in groups amongst the fields and in the lanes, but few close to the house. The Reader had come some way to meet us, and informed us that the priest had been that morning all over the place, warning the people not to meet me, and threatening all the terrors of the Church's curse to those who disobeyed. This seemed to account for the scattering of the people, as we could well imagine that the clashing of the priest's curse with the people's curiosity and desire would produce such an effect. We scarcely expected to find any children in the old building, but we went on, and arrived at the door.

When I looked in through the door I was astonished at the sight. The whole floor was crowded with little girls, as my witty and excellent friend Bishop Gregg said of a similar case, "as close as a barrel of herrings." When I went up the ladder sufficiently high to look into the upper floor, I found it equally well packed, but those who resembled the herrings were little boys. I came down and bid the Reader to bring out all the children into the open space before the building, and to count them as they came out. There were 154.

A wooden chair was brought, upon which I stood, and the children sat on the ground all round me. Then I told the Reader to call in some of the people who were standing about, but drawing nearer and nearer, as it were in spite of themselves. It was not easy to induce some of the first to come into the rough inclosure which at some distance surrounded the building; but when a few had ventured, others followed, until I had a considerable congregation.

The Reader had been speaking to them in Irish, and in the meantime I had been talking in loving words to the children. The adults seemed to sort themselves by sexes, for the women came up close to the children, most of them squatting upon the ground, while the men stood in the outer circle. I opened my pocket Bible, and read a short passage, which I bid the Reader who stood by me to give out in Irish. I then put up that little prayer, the use of which has been so often blessed, "Oh, God, for Christ's sake, give me thy Holy Spirit." And having acquired a tolerably correct pronunciation of the words in Irish, I repeated it in that language. This produced an effect which drew the loose gathering into a more compact congregation.

I do not think I ever preached the gospel with more earnestness, or with a greater effort at plainness. And while I set Christ before them in the attraction of his tenderness, I did not fail to act upon the principle of drawing the contrast between his truth and Roman delusions. In my earnest effort at plainness, I used an expression which I should generally have avoided, and said, "The sacrifice of the Mass is a lie." I mention this because I cannot choose but anticipate here the result of some years which followed this preaching. Eight years afterwards I was permitted to preach to a larger congregation in that same Sellerna, when the Lord's Supper was administered, and the Bishop of the Diocese was present. After the service, the Missionary who had been ordained to minister to the convert flock there was talking to me as we were surrounded by a crowd of the people. He called out from them eight individuals by name, and told me that these, who had been amongst the communicants, were some of the most consistent converts of the congregation; and that every one of them traced the beginning of the light which had brought them out of the darkness of Rome and enabled them to lay hold of the salvation of Christ, to the words they had heard at that first preaching by the walls of the old storehouse. One woman said that that expression to which I have alluded clung to her so, that she trembled whenever she went to Mass afterwards, and never rested until she found the truth in the Scriptures.

I closed my simple address by telling them that if they would agree to send their children, and to attend themselves to the teaching of the Holy Scriptures, we would build them a school-house and send them teachers. And remembering the success of such a proposal which I have described in telling of Castelkerke, I asked them to express their assent by holding up their hands. There were two men standing a little apart, and the Reader had told me that one was the priest's clerk, and the other his companion. When these men found what I was about to say, they spoke something in Irish which I did not understand. The heads of the band of men that encircled the seated women had gradually drawn so closely together, that it seemed but one mass of faces, and it was hard to say where their bodies could be packed. At the words of the priest's men these faces all turned round, and there was a burst of some expressions in Irish. The two men slunk away, and the faces formed again into their compact condition, with an expression that was highly interesting and encouraging. I bid the Reader put my words into Irish, and it drew forth a general show of hands, with a murmur of something which I learnt afterwards was approbation.

This was the commencement of the Mission at Sellerna. The Christian tourist that finds his way into that desolate district now, will see there a church capable of containing 500 worshippers, a school-house filled with intelligent scholars, and a neat and comfortable parsonage house, the residence of the Missionary-incumbent of a parochial district, endowed with an income partly from a Christian Society, and partly by the Ecclesiastical Commissioners. What hath God wrought! To Him be the glory of this blessed change.

CHAPTER XIII.

The progress of our spiritual adventure in the West of Ireland during the year 1848 was most encouraging, and every step tended to justify the original impression concerning the state of the people. The readiness with which the people attended upon the occasions afforded them, gave a prospect of future important results, and the countenance the movement received from the Bishop strengthened us in our efforts to induce the Irish Society of London to undertake direct and open Missionary work. The incidents already recorded laid the foundation for Missionary stations which have become important centers, and have manifested the blessing given to the work in a remarkable degree.

In order to enable the reader to judge of this blessing in the places where the present result has been specially eminent, it will be well to give the details of some of the beginnings, more particularly as they will convey a clearer view of the working of Divine Providence in raising the Irish Church Missions to their historical position with reference to the Church in Ireland. The events of a single day which happened to be crowded with circumstances of interest will contribute some materials for the history of the Church in a large district called Errismore; and will, besides, illustrate the nature of the operations by which the Missionary work was commenced, and by which that seed was sown in tears of which we are now reaping in joy the first sheaves of a large harvest.

Many months after the preaching at Sellerna described in the last chapter, and when the promised school there had been built, I was on a visit at Clifden Castle. My friend, the Rev. John Lynch, was there also, and it was arranged that we should visit the school at Errislanon, and endeavour to gather the people there that I might address them. We set forth early, and crossed the bay to the promontory of Errislanon, which is one of those slender fingers that make Connemara resemble a vast hand of earth laid upon the waters of the Atlantic. On arriving at the school we found the children and a number of adults standing about the door. The famine of 1847 had not yet left the land, though it had decreased, and its ravages had been checked by the bounty which had made such great efforts to supply the people with food. But its retirement only made room for the advance of the scourge which followed in its train; pestilence, cholera, and sad diseases were gathering the lives that famine had scarcely spared, and the general appearance of the people was truly deplorable.

I was addressing a group of men, women, and children thus marked with misery, and I was placing before them the comforting power of Christ's gospel as contrasted with the hardness of Rome's requirements, when a man came along the road in haste, and coming up to me, put a paper into my hand. It was a petition from the inhabitants of Errismore, asking that a school might be established in their district. It concluded with these words, "We are, therefore, willing to submit to a course of education based on the Scriptures; therefore, your kindness to afford us such facility for the improvement of our children shall be thankfully received and anxiously attended to, no matter what the opposition may be."

To this petition were appended 163 names.

Opposite to each was written the number of children the signer had to send, and these added together amounted to 439.

The petition and all the names were written in the same handwriting, and I asked the messenger who it was that had written it all. He said it was himself. Upon further inquiry, he assured me that every name was that of an individual who had authorized him to put it down. I asked, " Where is Errismore ?" He pointed across another bay to the south—that was Errismore, and the principal village was Derrygimla, which was close to the shore.

I bade the man (whose name was Stephen King) to go back to Derrygimla and gather as many as he could of those who had signed the petition; and I told him that I would cross the bay, and meet him by the time that he had reached Derrygimla by land. He bounded off at a hind's pace to make the circle of the road, in the hope of anticipating my straighter path across the water.

When I had closed my address to the people at the Errislanon School, we walked across the promontory, and arrived at a point where the Board of Works had authorized the expenditure of some money in the making of a pier, for the sake of employing the people.

There were about a dozen poor famished creatures who were nominally at work, but hardly moving one stone in a quarter of an hour. We had sent for the boat to go round from Clifden Bay to Mannin Bay, and we waited at this point for its arrival. It was impossible to lose the opportunity of telling the gospel to these apparently dying men, whose emaciated appearance gave me the most solemn impression as they stood or sat around me like living skeletons; and they listened with fixed attention, as if they were pausing on the brink of the grave to receive a message from heaven as to their journey beyond it. I do not remember that I ever set forth the salvation of Christ under so strong a feeling that my hearers would soon be called to experience the truth of my statement. As I stepped into the boat, I prayed earnestly for that group of hearers, who had heard the call of the gospel probably for the first time, and still more probably for the last time. None can tell how many of them had responded to the invitation and laid hold of Christ, who had so ordered his Providence that it should be sent to them even at the last moment, the eleventh hour of their lives.

We soon crossed the bay, and ran the boat upon a lovely beach of coral sand on the Errismore side. As Mr. D'Arcy was lame, I left him with Mr. Lynch, and pushed on at a brisker pace than theirs along the road towards the village of Derrygimla. I was overtaken by a woman with whom I entered into conversation, in which I found that her forefathers had been brought to the country as Protestants, but that the generations that followed had become Romanists. I was led to this by asking her name, which sounded Protestant and English—it was Wickham.

This brought me to the village, at the entrance of which stood the Chapel, a poor thatched building. Opposite to it was a decent house, and in the front of it a considerable number of people were waiting in groups, scattered amongst the large stones that formed the approach. This point was the object of Mrs. Wickham's journey, and she explained to me that the people were expecting the Relieving Officer, who came to that house to make his weekly administration of relief to the poor. I passed through the people, many of whom were squatting on the ground, and found my way to the highest large stone in the place, on which I stood, and asked in a loud voice, what they came there for. "For relief," was the reply. "I have got relief for you," I said; and the words brought the scattered groups into a closer crowd around me.

Speaking slowly and plainly, I said, "Man shall not live by bread alone, but by every word of God—that is, God's own Word." I went on to explain the power of the Scripture when applied by the Holy Spirit; told them of Christ as the Bread of Life—and, pointing to the Chapel just opposite, I declared that the bread of the Mass was not the Bread of Life." Mr. D'Arcy and Mr. Lynch had arrived as I was speaking, and stood amongst the hearers; and presently Stephen King also made his appearance, out of breath with his rapid journey round the head of the bay.

He made his way through the crowd, and coming up to me, he again put the petition into my hands. I opened the paper, and told the people what King had said to me; I called out some of the names subscribed, several of whom answered as being present, and acknowledged that they authorized their signatures to be placed to the petition. I then put it to the whole of the people whether, if a Schoolmaster were sent, they would take advantage of the instruction. There was a general assent, and I told them to select two men from amongst them, who should be authorized to arrange with me as to the place and other particulars. This was soon done, and two men at once conferred with us on the subject. The first point was as to a house in which to have a school. After various suggestions, it was remembered that there was a very large cabin which had been occupied as a hospital some years before, and had never been used since. To this we went, and found that it might be suitable for a schoolroom. Then we went to the owner, whom we found at some little distance off, and the visit to him ended by my engaging to rent the house. But it afforded no convenience for a habitation, being only one large room. We did not, however, depart until we had seen a proper place in which a Schoolmaster could be lodged. This being arranged, I promised that a Schoolmaster should be sent *soon* to begin the instruction.

We had sent from Errislanon a message to Clifden, desiring that a car should meet us at Derrygimla. It had arrived by the time we had completed the arrangement, and we three set forth upon it to go to Clifden. Our conversation turned at once upon the difficulty of finding a Schoolmaster to perform my promise, and the limit that was to be put upon the word *soon,* which I had used. "We must pray to God to send us a proper man," was the conclusion to which we came, and during a large portion of our drive to Clifden, the hearts of all three of us were lifted to the Throne of grace for this special object.

We drove up to the Hotel at Clifden, where we had ordered dinner; a number of persons were standing round the door. One came up to me while I was still on the car, and gave me a letter. It was from Colonel Thompson, the proprietor of an estate some eighteen miles off. He wrote to me to send me a man named Thomas Moran, whom he had employed for some time as a Schoolmaster, but he said that the difficulties of the times made it impossible for him to keep him on, and he asked me if I could employ him, as he could heartily recommend him. I got off the car and took Moran into the Hotel; and before we sat down to our dinner, it was arranged that this man should be the Schoolmaster at Errismore, and that he should go to Derrygimla, and collect the children to begin the school two days after, on the following Thursday. Then a man was forthwith despatched to Derrygimla, to announce the fact, and to bid the people to send the children on the appointed day.

Here was a prompt answer to the earnest prayers offered on the car as we had driven along. It seemed like the angel's word to Daniel, "at the beginning of thy supplication the commandment went forth." We received it as a token that the blessing would be given—a token which has been abundantly fulfilled. We had settled to dine at Clifden, because it had been arranged that we should visit the new school-house at Sellerna, and the people had been told to expect us. We hastened our meal and set out for Sellerna.

Streamstown is a scattered village, a couple of miles from Clifden. Streamstown Bridge was a favourite rendezvous for the faction-fights of the district; when we came to it we found several people leaning on the parapet of the bridge, or lounging about in the idleness that is produced by misery and desolation. We stopped the car, and I spoke to them, pointing them to the true and only source of comfort in Christ. This was the fourth congregation I had the opportunity to lead to Christ that day. We passed on, and in little more than a mile we came to a good-sized farm-house, in the yard of which there were assembled just such a gathering of poor starving creatures as we had seen at Derrygimla. They were waiting for the Relieving Officer, who was coming his rounds that day. It was impossible to pass by them, so I got off the car and repeated to them the blessed news of the gospel, which I had already announced to so many that day. They listened with marked attention, and without any sign of opposition, to the plain teaching that Christ is the only, and the all-sufficient Saviour.

While I was addressing these people, a man passed on the road, driving before him a horse, on the body of which were tied five roughly made coffins, two on each side, and one on the top. The sight gave an affecting tone to the words with which I closed my address. These coffins were being taken to the little villlage of Emlough—the same by the side of which our new school-house was built. We passed this distressing load and proceeded to that village. Here we found that the inhabitants had been suddenly attacked with cholera, and several had died after a few hours' illness. A panic had seized upon the people, and every living soul had deserted the place except two persons, a man and a woman. The panic-stricken people were Romanists; these two were converts. They had remained, and had done their utmost to tend the sick and dying, who were deserted by their own relations. It was a blessed testimony to the power of true religion to overcome the superstition and selfishness which characterizes the teaching of Rome.

We went into the new school-house, and found a goodly number awaiting us. Here again the Word that is able to save the soul was preached to the thirsting people, who appeared to drink in the living water, and it may be hoped that the Holy Spirit applied it in power to some of their hearts. This was a day much to be remembered in the annals of the preparation for the Irish Church Missions.

On the Thursday appointed, Thomas Moran set forth from Clifden to enter upon his work at Derrygimla. After passing the bridge at Ballinaboy the road is lonely, and advantage was taken of this in a manner similar to the attempt to stop the early work at Sellerna. Two men fell upon Moran when no one seemed to be within sight, and gave him a sound beating. When they left him, the poor fellow was sitting on the road, and he found that a woman who had seen the assault had hid herself in a part of the bog from fright, and now came to console him. By a little clever management Moran got from this woman the names of his assailants and her own name, and he made his way back to Clifden, applied to the stipendiary magistrate, before whom he swore informations, and the men were summoned to the court on Saturday, and the woman as a witness. When the case came, the men were convicted and sentenced to a heavy fine as damages, which Thomas Moran refused to take, and freely forgave them in the presence of the magistrates.

On the Thursday the people of Errismore had sent about fifty children to go to school. But the cause of the Schoolmaster's non-appearance was soon known, and the Errismore parents were very indignant. They feared that they might be supposed to be the parties who instigated the outrage upon Moran, and they sent two men to Clifden Castle to assure me that they had nothing to do with the matter, and that they would take care that the Schoolmaster should be safe at Derrygimla. I promised that the school should commence on Monday, on which day Moran went forth to his work accompanied by an agent in whom I had confidence. On arriving he found no fewer than 420 children who had collected from all parts of the district, and the parents of some of them who said they were quite willing that their children should be made Protestants. This was the result of the feeling produced by the attack on Moran. The Schoolmaster was greatly embarrassed by the number of scholars, and while he was taking down their names he sent the agent to me to ask what was to be done. The children were divided according to the villages from whence they came; and after some time four schools were opened, at Aillebrack, Duholla, Ballinaboy, and Derrygimla, each of which was well filled. Before long convenient school-houses were built in these several localities, and at the end of nineteen years all those schools are still carried on, well supplied with scholars, after several generations of children have received instruction and passed on to maturity.

Let any Christian tourist follow the course of our Missionary journey on the eventful day when the work began in Errismore, and he will find in the year 1867 that at Errislanon, besides the original school-house, there is a neat Church, and also the beginning of a parsonage-house, now in the course of erection. Let him cross Mannin Bay, and at Derrygimla he will see a handsome Church and a large school-house and a comfortable parsonage. Then let him visit the four schools and examine the children whom he will find occupying each. Let him pass on to Streamstown, and observe a picturesque school-house, where children are taught in the week, and where a congregation worship God on the Lord's-day. Let him go on to Sellerna, I need not repeat what in the last chapter I said he would find there. These are the fruits which God's blessing has brought forth from the little seed, the sowing of which has been described.—To God be the glory.

CHAPTER XIV.

THE details of the work already given will be enough to show that much blessing had accompanied all the efforts hitherto made. They will also manifest that the original expectation as to the state of the people's mind was fully justified. These successes strengthened the desire for a more extensive and general work amongst the Roman Catholics, and settled our conviction that open missionary operations, carried on upon the principles already set forth, were required, and would be successful.

It has been stated more than once that there was no intention of forming any new organization for this missionary work; indeed, Mr. Durant very strongly opposed such a notion. It was felt by us both that the Irish Society afforded a machinery already at work, which only required to be developed so as to include operations of the nature we proposed, and that its general acceptance with the Irish Clergy would greatly further the plan. This rendered our disappointment the greater when we found the repugnance of the leading members of that Society to the desired extension of their original scheme. Mr. Durant was often much moved when I reported to him the earnest conversations I had from time to time with the excellent men who conducted the affairs of that Society. The objections they stated, and their rejection of the testimony we offered as to the prepared condition of the people's mind, led us to a repeated examination of our views and our hopes; and as these were always more confirmed by such examination, the opposition we met with tended to strengthen our resolution to proceed.

There existed at that time a Society called the Irish Society of London. It was formed in 1822, about four years after the Irish Society in Dublin. This Society was in the habit of remitting a large portion of its funds to the Irish Society in Dublin, to carry on its work; but in other respects it acted as an independent Society. Mr. Durant was a member of its committee, and I joined it in

April, 1846. We both of us endeavoured, at that early date, to impress upon the members of the committee the views which we entertained as regards the necessity of open missionary operations. These were not readily received at first, but the letters to the "Morning Herald," to which reference has been made, were approved, and printed for circulation. Towards the end of the year 1846 Mr. Durant was anxious to infuse a more missionary feeling into the committee, and at his suggestion a resolution was passed, inviting the Reverends Edward Bickersteth, Montague Villiers, and Baptist Noel to join the committee and attend its meetings. None of these accepted the invitation except Edward Bickersteth, who from that time gave earnest attention to the work in hand.

We had already prevailed upon the committee to sanction an appeal to produce a separate fund for Missionary efforts, which were not to be carried on by the ordinary income of the Society. This appeal had only produced a balance of £90 over its necessary expenses when Mr. Bickersteth joined the committee, and he was asked to prepare another appeal. This he did, but it was considered to be of too general a character on behalf of education to suit the objects of the Irish Society; and the members present, while rejecting it in connection with the Society, formed themselves into a separate committee for sending it forth.

A very important event took place immediately after this, in December, 1846. One of the energetic ladies so often referred to in the early chapters had formed an Association for employing Scripture-Readers, called the Ladies' Auxiliary to the Irish Society. This Association was bound by its parent committee not to make public appeals, but to gather funds by friendly correspondence. Its operations by Scripture-Readers were carried on entirely by these means, as they had no share of the funds of the Irish Society. The work of the Ladies' Auxiliary was a step in advance of that of the Irish Society, the efforts of which were directed to what was termed "the mechanical teaching of the Scriptures." The judgment of Miss Mason perceived that the instruction to read the Irish Scriptures needed a further step wherever it was successful. Her earnest zeal overcame the difficulties in her way, and she took the step in advance which she could not induce others to take. With indefatigable diligence she gathered the means of supporting her few Scripture-Readers. When a proposal was made in a committee of the Irish Society of London to make a grant to the Ladies' Auxiliary it produced much discussion, which, however, terminated in making a grant of £300. This was done at a full meeting of committee, and by a fair majority; but at the next meeting of committee, the few who assembled for routine business did not confirm that particular minute. The members of that separate committee above mentioned, on being informed of this, came to the rescue of the original resolution, which was finally confirmed on the 6th of January, 1847, and the grant was remitted to the Ladies' Auxiliary. This produced much and difficult correspondence between the two Societies, which lasted a considerable time. In September, 1847, this correspondence led to the necessity for holding a conference with the committee in Dublin. I went, accompanied by another member of the committee, and we were charged with distinct instructions as regards the standing and position of the Irish Society of London. It was a friendly conference, such as should be carried on between Christian men who commence their discussions by seeking the help of God in prayer. There were several points which rendered it a difficult duty, which, however, was conscientiously discharged on both sides.

The nature of the conversations which took place, as well as their result, may be gathered from the minutes which were passed by the committee of the London Irish Society on the 28th of October, 1847, after we had made our report. They are as follows:—

792. "This Committee, having taken into their consideration the connection between the two Societies in London and Dublin, feel satisfied that the Irish Society of London, in the first public formation, from the general tenor of its accounts, and from the published rules and regulations, is an independent Society, formed with the same view and object as the Irish Society of Dublin."

793. "Resolved, that although formed an independent Society, yet the Irish Society of London has hitherto remitted a considerable portion of its funds to the Irish Society of Dublin, for the payment of their Inspectors, Teachers, and General Expenses; and viewing the great work which, under the blessing of the Most High, has been carried on through the instrumentality of the Irish Society, this Committee do not see any occasion for departing from the practice above mentioned in the ordinary business of the Society, but without confining itself to that work alone."

While the correspondence between the two

Societies was going on, the separate committee which had grown out of the Irish Society of London, and had circulated Mr. Bickersteth's appeal, had taken a form, and become an independent body. After several consultations it assumed the name of "The Special Fund for the Spiritual Exigences of Ireland."

Many of the members were anxious to arrange a plan by which the committee itself migh tset on foot direct Missionary work in Ireland; but several difficulties arose, and much was urged against such a plan, and at last the committee laid down a fundamental rule that they would only act in supporting Societies which were already existing and in operation in Ireland. The pressure of the famine, then impending and already commencing its desolation, was likely to divert the sources of supply from the Societies whose aim was the spiritual benefit of the people, and therefore the assistance of generous Christians in England would be of essential importance in maintaining them. The committee of the "Special Fund" therefore limited their grants to existing spiritual associations. The money was liberally contributed, and in January, 1847, they issued the following statement, which sufficiently explains their position :—

"The Special Fund for the Spiritual Exigences of Ireland is in no way connected with any means of relieving the temporal wants of the Irish. The individual contributors to this Fund have acted in other ways, and by other instrumentality, in endeavouring to relieve the present great distress; but, whichever of them has done this (and doubtless all have), the Committee of the Special Fund are in no way connected with any machinery for supplying food, or temporal benefits of any kind.

"The Special Fund makes no attempt whatever for the formation of new machinery of any kind to meet the spiritual exigences of Ireland. The only object is to be the channel of communicating to the Societies, already existing and in operation in Ireland, the pecuniary assistance which English Christians are ready to give. Under the circumstances which are now pressing so heavily upon the resources of Ireland, without such help those Societies could neither hope to carry on their ordinary work, which has been already so greatly blessed, nor to extend their operations to meet the increased requirements for their efforts. These requirements are very large, and arise both from the peculiar preparation which the existing misery has made amongst the Irish of all religions, and also from the special demand for Scriptural instruction, so striking at the present time, as emanating from a large proportion of the Roman Catholics themselves.

In carrying out these principles, the Committee of the Special Fund have already made grants to the Irish Society for both its branches of labour, the Church Education Society, the Scripture-Readers' Society, and the Additional Curates' Fund."

The circumstances which have been detailed in this chapter were occurring while the events recorded in the previous chapters were continually strengthening Mr. Durant and myself in the conviction that our great object must be attained. Every progressive step in the West made it more plain that the work was of God, and gave us courage to persevere.

When it was necessary to abandon the hope that the Irish Society in Dublin would adopt the open Missionary principle, Mr. Durant turned all his energy to induce the Irish Society of London to do this. The difficulties that arose there led him to look to the Special Fund Committee with hope; and, in the expectation that the London Society would carry. out Missionary operations with the funds of this Special Committee, he consented to the limitation they imposed on themselves, and the more readily from his strong disinclination to originate a new organization. He laboured in the two committees in London towards this end, and at length, in the month of June, 1847, a resolution was passed by the committee of the London Irish Society, that they would undertake direct Missionary work in Ireland, with money supplied to them by the committee of the Special Fund, and without reference to the Dublin Society. This opens the way for an account of the manner in which this arrangement was carried out, which shall occupy the next chapter.

CHAPTER XV.

It was a very great advance when the Irish Society of London agreed to carry on Missionary work in Ireland, and when the committee of the Special Fund agreed to supply them with the means; it gave us a vantage ground from which there was every prospect of more enlarged success. The feeling of a large number of the Irish clergy were awakened to the necessity for such a movement. This was tested in a striking manner. In January, 1847, the Rev. Thomas Vores suggested a plan for sending relief to the famishing people in Ireland, which was acted upon to some extent, and produced very beneficial results. He proposed that the clergyman of one parish in England should put himself into communication with the clergyman of one parish in Ireland—that the English flock should contribute towards the support of the Irish flock, receiving from the Irish clergyman authentic reports of the weekly condition of the people, upon which reports the next week's contributions were raised in the English parish. The execution of this scheme was entrusted mainly to the committee of the Irish Society of London, which gave publicity to the plan, received the applications, and put the parties in communication with each other. There were 94 applications from clergymen in England to be placed in correspondence with a parish in Ireland; and there were 250 applications from Irish clergymen to receive the benefit. Of the 250, no fewer than 124 asked to have the services of a Scripture-Reader for Missionary work amongst their Roman Catholic parishioners.

Grants were made by the Special Fund Committee for particular cases. It was thus that a salary was allowed to Mr. O'Callaghan for his work at Castelkerke, which has been recorded; and in January, 1848, the Irish Society of London voted an increased salary to him, which was necessary to secure his ordination.

Gradually the minds of the good men engaged in these two committees opened to perceive the real nature of the work in the west of Ireland, and they consented to the extension of Missionary work. A sum was voted for a Mission in the town of Galway, and two active Agents were sent there, who laid the foundation of much success, which followed at a later and more mature state of the work. A grant was also made for a Mission at Clifden, by which some Agents and Schoolmasters were appointed, who worked under the superintendence of Mr. Hyacinth D'Arcy, with the permission of the absent rector and the resident curate, the Rev. M. A. Foster. These operations were carried on under the direction of Mr. Durant and myself. The funds were supplied by the Special Committee, and the nominal responsibility rested in the Irish Society of London.

In April, 1848, I obtained a grant and permission to commence a Mission at a place called Rooveagh, in the southern part of the County of Galway. The origin of that Mission is so remarkable, and has led to such consequences, that it requires to be stated at some length.

At the end of 1847 and beginning of 1848, I heard of the conversion of a Roman priest, which made some noise in Dublin. He had been received by the Priests' Protection

Society some time before, and was then living in Dublin, without any occupation, and exposed to much persecution in the form of calumny, and much distress from the small means that could be allowed him for support. He was introduced to me, and I had several conversations with him. My experience of Roman priests, both abroad and in Ireland, was not calculated to induce me readily to trust them. The manner of preparing the mind of a youth, and the training by which his character is formed and hardened for the peculiar work of the Roman priesthood, make it very difficult to soften it again into a fitness for the Christian ministry. This is peculiarly the case in the colleges in Ireland, and more especially at the College at Maynooth. My knowledge of this training, and the intercourse which I had occasionally with some priests of the Roman Church, did not dispose me to give a favourable reception to the convert in question. But there was a frankness in his manner, and an openness in his way of communicating his case that attracted me, and led me to make more inquiries than I had been inclined to do at first.

I found that he had not been brought up at Maynooth, that he was a native of the

County of Galway, and had gone out to Canada, where he was educated for the priesthood, and ordained to minister among the French Romanists there; that he had returned to Ireland, and had become the Roman Catholic curate of his native place. His account of his conversion was extremely interesting, and his manner of relating it gave me an impression of truthfulness. I well knew that the usual mode of treating a priest who showed any tendency towards Protestant doctrine was to asperse his character, and therefore it did not surprise me that such a course was taken in this case; but I took every means to ascertain the truth of what was said against him, and I could find no sufficient reason to justify the charges. Every time I conversed with him I was drawn more and more to take a favourable view of his case; and I began to hope that he might have been providentially brought into communication with me, in order to be made an instrument in carrying on the great work we were contemplating.

But the more I felt this, the stronger I considered the necessity of proving the sincerity and capacity of this convert by some very strong test; and, after prayerful consideration, I did suggest to him a proof calculated to try him to the utmost. He had for a long time been the Roman Catholic priest of the village of Rooveagh, where his relations resided. He had been very active in the discharge of his duties there. The large village of Craughwell within his district had no chapel, and he had determined to build one. He had diligently gathered contributions for this purpose, and carried on the building as the money came in. It was intended to be a more decent edifice than the chapels in the neighbourhood, and the walls were raised six or seven feet high, when, while waiting for more funds for his building, more light was given to his own mind. I remember to have seen the unfinished building in travelling by the road from Loughrea to Galway. The active priest, who had carried on the work so far, had been obliged to escape from the dangers which threatened him on leaving the Church of Rome. I was acquainted with the rector of the parish, and knew something of the locality, and I made up my mind to propose to this convert-priest that he should undertake a Mission at Rooveagh.

The conversation in which I made this proposition will not easily pass from my memory. I talked to him of the value of a testimony for Christ among the same people where, in days of ignorance, a man had given a testimony against Him. I referred to the scriptural account of the early confessors of the truth, and when I had prepared the way in this manner, I asked him whether he felt courage enough to undertake a Christian and Scriptural mission to the same people to whom he had administered the Mass. I told him that if he would go to Rooveagh on such an errand, I would go with him and support him; that I would give him the assistance of two Agents, and visit the Mission myself at every emergency. He was agitated as I went on detailing my proposition, interspersing my statement with scriptural assurances of the protecting hand of God by his Providence, and of the comforting support of his Holy Spirit. He told me that I was sending him to martyrdom —that I did not know the positive danger into which I wished him to rush—that all the power of the priests would be exercised against him, with all the submissive fanaticism of the people for their agency. I assured him that I was fully aware of the danger, but that I also knew the power of God, and added that I had no other employment to offer him, but that I would undertake a Mission at Rooveagh if he would undertake to conduct it. I closed the conversation by telling him that I did not wish him to decide upon an impulse, and that therefore he should take time to consider the matter. We then knelt down together, and I commended him to God earnestly in prayer, specially asking for that wisdom which is promised to all that seek it by Him who "giveth to all men liberally, and upbraideth not."

I confess that I had expected that my proposal would be rejected, while I felt that nothing less than the severest test would justify me in engaging the services of one who had been a Roman Catholic priest. I was encouraged to hope that this was a true man and a true Christian by the manner in which he did not reject my proposal, and I continued my prayer that he might be guided aright in his decision. I had not to wait long. On the next morning at eight o'clock, I was dressing myself at an hotel in Dublin, when I was told that a gentleman wished to see me. "Let him come up," and my convert friend appeared in my bed-room. He spoke with great emotion, and told me that he had not closed his eyes all night, and that after much prayer he had made up his mind to agree to my proposal—to cast himself upon God and do his best, though he fully believed that nothing short of divine interference could save his life. I warmly encouraged him, and thanking God, we knelt again, and solemnly committed the Rooveagh Mission to his special care and blessing.

On my return to England, I stated the case to the two committees in London, and was, in February 1848, authorized by them to take steps for commencing the proposed Mission. The preparations were made, and in the following April I went down to Rooveagh with my convert priest. I have avoided mentioning his name till now, as all who know anything of the present state of the Irish Church Missions would have anticipated the result on reading the name of the Rev. Roderick Ryder. He is now the efficient and diligent incumbent Missionary of Errismore in Connemara, and has long been an active minister in the great work of the Missions.

The difficulties that attended this Mission may be easily imagined, though it would not be easy to detail them. I felt that Mr. Ryder required especial countenance and encouragement, and I gladly made every effort to afford them to him. I visited Rooveagh as often as I could, and I found that while my expectations of the opposition were fully realized, my best hopes were not disappointed. Mr. Ryder went to work judiciously as well as actively. The clan feeling of his relatives in the place was of some advantage, and the surprise of the people to find their former priest inviting them to read the Scriptures, often counterbalanced the dread of their present priest's curse. It may be enough to relate the circumstances which occurred in the autumn of 1848, not six months after Mr. Ryder's appearance as a missionary at Rooveagh, to convey a just impression of the effect he had produced, and the progress he had made.

At that time Mr. Ryder reported that there were between forty and fifty persons to whom he and the Agent had been teaching the Scriptures, and who were willing to learn of them in spite of the denunciations of the priests. I asked him whether he thought he could bring them together to meet me on a certain day, and let me address them, and examine them as to the knowledge they had attained. He wrote in answer that he thought he could. The day was fixed, and I went to Rooveagh to keep my appointment.

When I arrived I found the people already gathered awaiting me. They were assembled in the loft of a barn, to which the only access was by a ladder. There were about forty persons present; most of them had Bibles or Testaments. They read for me verse after verse, and answered well the questions I put to them respecting salvation in Christ and Christ alone. They all spoke Irish; and while I endeavoured to accommodate my English to their idioms, I put in a word or two of Irish which I had learned, and I remember that an interesting discussion took place with reference to the Irish word which I had used to signify Christ as a "Substitute." This brought out an amount of knowledge which satisfied me that the Missionary work had not been neglected. I thanked God, and took courage, and after about an hour and a half's conference with them they joined me in prayer, and I dismissed them.

I continued talking with Ryder for some time in the loft, when a man came up the ladder in haste and alarm, telling us that the priest was "down there in the road terrifying the people." We hastened down, and on getting into the road we saw the priest on horseback, with his hunting-whip in his hand, a few yards from a man who stood with his back close to a wall, while the priest was scolding him; a few other people were standing about, evidently terrified, and as if they were mesmerised with fear. Mr. Ryder went up to a small group at a short distance, and I went to the place where the priest was abusing the man. Taking my position between the two, I addressed the man, and told him that he had no need to be ashamed of having attended to the reading of God's own Word, as it contained the only account of the means by which his soul could be saved. I was proceeding to give a very brief but plain statement of that salvation, which I intended for the benefit of the priest as much as for the man, when the priest, who had said nothing while I was speaking, suddenly turned his horse, and gallopped off at full speed; upon which a shout and laughter burst forth from a number of persons whose heads then appeared above the low loose stone walls, behind which they had crouched to hide themselves when the priest had made his appearance.

On looking for Ryder, I saw that several persons had gathered round him, and there was evidently some strong altercation. I immediately went up to him, and as I came near, all the people walked away except two or three. One of these was a man who was returning from his work, and carried a scythe over his shoulder. He had been the person who had produced the altercation, and his countenance was full of anger; his compressed lip and lowering eye sufficiently told what was passing within. I first spoke to Ryder and then to this man, very gently remonstrating with him, remembering that "a soft answer turneth away wrath." I had not spoken many words when he deliberately brought down his scythe from his shoulder, and held it as in the act of mowing, with one step forward. I do not think that I was ever in greater danger in Ireland than at this moment. An instant thought of prayer for protection went up to the Throne of grace, and knowing well the temper of the Irish, I stood quite still, and without any anger in my countenance, I looked him full in the face, eye to eye. After a pause in this position, his eye and his scythe dropped together; he put it again over his shoulder, and walked away. I thanked God for what I believed to be a real preservation from serious danger. I feel sure that had I shown any fear, or attempted to move away, this excited man would have cut me down. Impress upon an Irishman that you are not afraid of him, and you are safe with him.

The Mission at Rooveagh went on under Mr. Ryder's superintendence, and I doubt not that all the events of the day I have described tended in no small degree to confirm and establish him as a true missionary in the minds of the people. Before the close of the year 1848 there was a marked progress and much encouragement in every one of the districts in which our Missionary efforts had been made. It was plainly a duty to go forward, but increasing difficulties were felt in the working of the central machinery in London. The difficulty became excessive, when the resources of the Special Fund for the Spiritual Exigences of Ireland decreased. In the year 1847 that fund was enabled to distribute amongst the religious societies in Ireland about £10,000; in 1848 it did not receive more than £5000. The occasion which had called it into existence had passed with the worst days of the famine, and the liberality which it had called forth was diverted into other channels. Hence it became impossible to make the necessary grants to the Irish Society of London for the special support of the Missionary work, which was likely to extend and make larger demands for funds, while the means of supplying them diminished. Besides this the complicated machinery by which the arrangement was carried on was no small impediment. Mr. Durant and myself were members of both committees; but while we were directing the work in Ireland it was no easy task, first to justify a grant of money for a particular object in the Special Committee, and then to justify its application in the committee of the Irish Society of London, where some of the members reluctantly concurred in the course that we were pursuing.

This was the state of matters in October, 1848, when I returned from a visit to Ireland, and brought very heartstirring reports of the progress of these early Missionary efforts. Taking all things into consideration, the committee of the Special Fund felt unanimously that the time was come for an independent machinery to carry on the work which was so evidently blessed—which it was impossible to forego—and as impossible to pursue with the instrumentality hitherto employed. Even Mr. Durant's strong objection to a new organization was overcome; and having failed to effect his great object of inducing either of the Irish Societies to undertake the open Missionary work, he heartily concurred in the decision of the Special Committee. Early in November, at a full meeting of the committee, this point was finally decided, and it was resolved that arrangements should be made for the formation of a Society, the object of which should be to carry on a Christian mission to the Roman Catholics of Ireland in connection with the Established Church. The arrangement of the details was to be submitted to a subsequent meeting of the committee, which would then transfer to the new Society whatever balance might remain in their hands.

It was about the middle of November that this decision was finally made; and as I walked from the meeting with Mr. Durant to his home in Mansfield Street, he expressed his heartfelt rejoicing that the great object of his desires was attained, and that we might rest satisfied that the Missionary work would now be carried on in a systematic manner, and, trusting to God's blessing, with a prospect of permanency. I left him to go home, after arranging with him to come up to London on the 22nd to prepare memoranda for the detail of the new Society. I heard no more of him till the appointed day, when I went to London, and on knocking at his door I asked his servant, "How is Mr. Durant?" as he had a bad cold when I parted from him. "He died this morning, sir," was the reply. My heart was stricken at the loss of this dear friend with whom I had worked in Christian love and harmony so long and in such important affairs; but I recognized the hand of God in the time when he was called to his rest. He was over eighty years of age, and for the last few years of his life Ireland had been laid upon his heart as he often said to me; and he had laboured and prayed for the spiritual benefit of Irish Roman Catholics with an earnestness and zeal which renewed, as it were, the spring-time of his Christian life. He was a man of single-hearted sincerity and strict conscientiousness. He had been raised up at a peculiar juncture for a special purpose, and as soon as that purpose was accomplished, he was called to the rest that remaineth for the people of God.

It was not until a meeting of the Special Committee on the 20th of March, 1849, that a separate committee was appointed to settle the rules and constitution and name of the new Society. These were finally arranged on the 29th of March, 1849, when the Society for Irish Church Missions to the Roman Catholics began its existence. An inaugural public meeting was held in the following May, when the officers and committee were formally appointed.

A list of the officers then appointed, and the Constitution, Object, and Rules of the Society then adopted, will be found in the Appendix.

This Story has now been brought to the point to which all the preparatory steps were tending, and it has been seen how the Society for Irish Church Missions has arisen into its present form and organization by the direct operation of Divine Providence.

The singular blessing which followed,—the rapid increase of the means supplied,—the remarkable supply of agents suited to the circumstances as they occurred,—together with the incidents which marked the progress of the work,—these will form the substance of the Second Part of the Story, in which it is proposed to set forth the history of the Society itself.

It is impossible to contemplate the results, as they are seen in the eighteenth year of the Society's existence, without admiring the Providential arrangements which brought them about. The outward and material evidence of the Lord's hand in the Society's operations are sufficient to indicate the greatness of his purpose. The building of twenty-one churches and eight parsonage-houses, of thirty school-houses and four Orphanages, are substantial witnesses of the reality of the work. All these have been erected for congregations gathered from a false communion to the worship of the Divine Saviour according to the truth of his Word, and for the rearing of children, who without them would have been brought up in delusions of a false creed. The controversy with Roman teaching has been proclaimed in the length and breadth of the land. The supine neglect of lukewarm Protestants has been aroused, and their ignorance has been enlightened. Large numbers of persons have left the Church of Rome; and as the highest and most glorious of the results of the Society's operations, very many have been so taught by the Holy Spirit, that in life and in death they have confessed the faith of Christ crucified, and adorned the doctrine of God their Saviour.

In reviewing the Providential preparation which led to these great results, several practical impressions force themselves upon the mind of a Christian reader, such as the following:—

1. The Almighty works by the weakest means in bringing about great results; and often rejects those which seem appropriate to the end, in order that the very inappropriate-

ness of those which are successful may draw the observation to Him with whom " it is nothing to conquer with many, or with them that have no power." No sense of weakness should deter from a work which the Providence of God places in our way.

2. "The hairs of your head are all numbered" indicates the minuteness of the events by which, as with a small rudder, the Almighty steers and alters the course of the greatest events. Of this the preceding pages afford abundant proof. It is the part of a wise man to watch for the pointings of Providence in what are considered the trifles of our daily life.

3. What is really of God, and has a purpose in the Divine mind, is often laid upon the heart of a Christian, and will not be cast aside. It rises from his heart, and occupies his mind. When this is the case, the matter is followed with a perseverance which looks like obstinacy. But such perseverance in such a cause is one token of certain success, and should be dealt with as they dealt with St. Paul's determination; "When he would not be persuaded, they said the will of the Lord be done." This Story shows again and again the power of an untiring perseverance in the Lord's work.

4. One of the most ordinary modes by which the Almighty distinguishes his purpose, is by planting a strong impulse to prayer for the object in the heart of his servants. He gives them, too, a spirit of expectancy in the growth of these plants of prayer. Whoever watches his prayers to wait for answers will find them fall about his path whenever he is walking in the way of the Lord. How many instances of this do these pages record! How many more might have been recorded had greater details been given.

5. But the most important practical lesson which may be drawn from this Story is the wonderful effect of a constant appeal to the power of the Holy Spirit in every passage, whether of lesser or of greater influence upon the Lord's work. Not one of the steps taken in all that has been recorded but was referred, openly as well as inwardly, to the direction of the Holy Spirit. The link that may be said to have bound the chain of Providences to the Almighty hand which worked them was the unvarying and unforgotten use of that blessed prayer, "O God, for Christ's sake, give the Holy Spirit."

APPENDIX.

The following are the two Tracts referred to in Chapter VI. :—

I.
A VOICE FROM HEAVEN TO IRELAND.

Surely Ireland is a fine country; her hills and her dales, her mountains and her rivers, are cast in the mould of beauty, and covered with a soil of fruitfulness: but look upon them in a moral point of view, and there seems a mist hovering over them that makes the heart sigh, even while the eye rejoices.

Surely the people of Ireland are a clever people; they seem to have been born thinking happy thoughts, and to have been nurtured in the habit of making them group together in the attitude of wit: but a melancholy feeling seems to fold up the smile that their wit produces—the talent is full and overflowing, but it runs to waste, or to work mischief.

Surely the hearts of the Irish are warm hearts, buoyant hearts, elastic as a steel spring, and as strong to love, without being so hard to feel; yet is there a sorrow about their love, and all their energy of heart is powerless. It works no mighty —no sustained work; there is no greatness in it.

What can be the cause of so strange a disappointment?—so fruitless an autumn from a spring of such blossom?

There is one giant cause for this distressing condition;—all minor hindrances are merged in that. IRELAND IS ENSLAVED—she is in bondage under a foreign yoke—a yoke of most merciless tyranny, and all the more reckless in its tyrant rule because it is thoroughly un-Irish, wholly foreign to the soil, to the blood, and to the feeling of Irishmen.

The peculiar feature of this foreign usurpation is, that it works deceitfully, under the mask of the Irish name, to enslave, not the soil, not the bodies, not the properties of Irishmen, but that which uses their soil, moves their bodies, and disposes of their properties. It enslaves their souls, places their consciences in bondage, and controls the very spirit of the man. An Italian ruler, governing a small district in temporal matters, has set up an unfounded claim to govern in spiritual matters the whole world, and every soul in it. He was originally the Christian Bishop of the diocese of Rome. In the darkness of ignorance, in which all Europe at one time lay, he fixed his fetters on the consciences of kings and of their people, boldly presuming to do this in the assumed name of Christ Himself; at the same time that he used the usurped power to seal up and lay aside the book of authority to which he pretended to refer for establishing his claim. This Italian put the yoke upon the neck, under the warrant of the book of which he showed but the outside, and forbade his foolish victims to search whether the warrant of God justified his ambitious claim.

The fathers, who first endured this Italian tyranny, have left the slavery as a legacy to their children; and tyrant after tyrant has risen up from generation to generation, even until now, when the consciences of men, cramped for centuries with the tight manacles that first wounded the soul, and then hardened the sore, dare not rise and think—dare not open the eye and see—dare not spring forth and act to throw off the terrible trammels.

But no wonder that the poor enslaved Irish are kept in the snare, and tremble at the thought of venturing to be free; for, in order to keep Irish hearts, the usurper has cunningly arranged a band of Italian police, who live among the Irish with the appearance of Irishmen. In order to effect this, the system is to take a young Irishman, and separate him from his family to place him under training, where all the special love of Ireland's liberty, and Ireland's hope, and Ireland's joy, is drafted out of his heart, and the vacancy filled up with Italian feelings and Italian characteristics; while an object is placed before his ambition, closely connected with the Italian supremacy, and absolutely involving Ireland's degradation. After transforming the Irish youth into this unnatural foreigner, when he has become Italianised, the usurper secures his agent from the return of natural and patriotic affections, by depriving him of the sources of Irish domestic feeling. He never can be under the temptation to feel for his original country again as a husband can feel for the people of a beloved wife—as a father can feel for the country of his children. All the possible avenues by which Irish feelings of affection might flow in to mitigate, in the least, his Italianised heart, are not only closed, but the gates that shut them up are barred with oaths; and if such feelings creep in through any crevice, conscience is scared with the alarm of "sin." Can these be called Irishmen, who have foresworn the links of Irish love—the ties of Irish domestic feeling, and have given themselves, body, soul, and spirit, to work the will of an Italian usurper in keeping the Irish people enslaved, and in hiding from them the Book of God that would set them free? No—these are no longer Irishmen, though their births were registered on the soil of Ireland. A poor Irishman would hold himself mocked if you gave him a potatoe from the outer skin of which all the mealy inside had been scooped, and every fibre, and every eye, had been cut off, so that it was neither good to eat nor to plant. You might tell him that the potatoe grew in Connaught, but he would not own it for a native root.

This Italian usurpation is the real foreign slavery of unhappy Ireland—the more depressing and terrible, because it fetters the soul, the spirit, and the source of action in the man, debases him, and cows his conscience; and leaves him without capacity to rise and ask for the document which proves the high warrant of God's Word, assumed by the tyrant. The debasing nature of this spiritual slavery can hardly be more clearly shown than by the cheat which is put upon the enslaved ones, to turn off their attention from the real usurper. The Italianised police boldly talk in terms that might seem to be suited to the real condition of slavery in which the Irish are kept; but these terms, which echo on the heart of the suffering slaves, are artfully misdirected to point to the political dominion of England as the cause of the evil, instead of the spiritual tyranny of the utterly foreign Italian. IRISHMEN! when will you open your eyes to see the cheat? Surely, in vain the net is spread in the sight of any bird.

There was a time when all the nations of Europe were in the same bondage to this Italian power as the Irish are now. Three hundred years ago the people of England, by God's help, and in God's strength, cast off their chains. They cried for the Book of God—they got it—they read it—and, by God's blessing, it dissolved the spell by which they had been bound. England became spiritually free, and the blessing of God has prospered her ever since.

But the truth must be told: England did not treat their brethren of this island as tenderly as they ought to have done; they tried to work a freedom for them which, under God, a people must work for themselves. The Irish rejected the forced freedom, and perpetuated the foreign slavery. It was a sad, a painful, a sinful mistake on the part of Englishmen. May God forgive them for it! Irish hearts must forgive them now; and whatever be the feelings that may rankle still, yet, IRISHMEN! be not so mad as to pursue your quarrel with your kindred, by fastening more closely the fetters of your foreign yoke. How absolutely foolish is the suicidal spite which would throw yourselves into a perpetual prison, to avoid shaking hands with your brother. He who profits by your alienation from the English is the Italian despot; and none suffer so severely as yourselves.

It is three hundred years ago since a voice from heaven sounded over England, and called the nation into the glorious liberty of the children of God. Some of its divine power was manifested in its success, but the call was echoed to Ireland in the harsher voice of man; and in passing from Holyhead to Howth it lost its power. Well, that time is gone by; and though the lost opportunity has entailed three centuries of sorrow upon Ireland, yet if she hearken now, she may hear the music of that voice again, sweeping across the heartstrings of Germany. In the former arousing to freedom, a large portion of the German people stood up and cast off the Italian tyranny! but there were multitudes who still lay prostrate with the tyrant's foot upon their necks, and their weakness then bequeathed to their children, in bondage and in bitterness of conscience, a legacy of sorrow similar to that of Ireland. But now there has risen up amongst them men upon whom the light of truth is beaming, and whose hearts and consciences are stirred up to spiritual honesty. They have found that the old fetters upon their consciences had rusted, and they fell off at a touch; and spiritual liberty has become the watchword which passes from city to city, and from town to town—yea, from village to village, in Germany, raising up thousands upon thousands, who claim the name of CHRISTIAN and of CATHOLIC, while they cast off the Antichristian usurpation of the Italian tyrant.

There are many marks in the great movement now proceeding in Germany which seem to tell of heavenly wisdom, of heavenly love, and of heavenly power, mixed, indeed, with the infirmity of man, but measured out through that pure vessel— the Word of God. There were ancient mistakes, and hereditary feelings, which would have made it unwise to attempt the joining of this infant liberty of conscience with the more matured and accustomed system which has grown for three hundred years under the name of Protestantism. In the rush by the German Catholics for an escape from the usurpation of Rome, there is no time for the adjustment of measures with the Churches of former freedom. Besides, they rise up as a nation, and as a nation give their name to the Church that is amongst them. IRISHMEN! what hinders the formation of the FREE IRISH CATHOLIC CHURCH, built upon the rock of truth by the working of the written Word of God? There is one only hindrance—the enslaved will of the Irish people, who, with their fathers, have been in bondage to the foreign despotism of an Italian priest. This points to the true application of those lines:—

> "Hereditary bondsmen, know ye not,
> Who would be free, himself must strike the blow?"

Whatever blow is struck in this cause must be by the heart of a Christian, wielding the Word of truth by the power of the Spirit of Christ. May that Spirit raise a host of such hearts to work for the glory of Christ, in SETTING IRELAND FREE!

If every Irishman who reads this, and feels his heart burn within him at the thought, were to carry that flaming torch at once to light his neighbour's heart, and he another's, and another's, there would presently be THOUSANDS OF BANDS of burning hearts, gathering together in cot and cabin—why not in palace and in parlour?—and many a word of counsel and of encouragement would pass from lip to lip; and such bands would go in quiet boldness, and with untrembling courage, in numbers to their priests. Calmly and firmly they would say—
"*We are* CATHOLIC CHRISTIANS—*we claim the power to read the written Word of God, in order that we may know Christ and his salvation for ourselves. We would worship God, but it must be in a language by which our own tongues can tell the feelings of our own hearts;—we refuse the rule of an Italian priest; we invite you, who have been his agent, to join us in our freedom, and to show that you yourself are free, by renouncing the evil oath that cut you off from domestic union with your native people, contrary to God's law; and by mixing amongst us as a husband, and ceasing to be separated to the Italian's system. Join us, and lead us in freedom of conscience; or leave us to the liberty to which we are called by the voice of God Himself.*"

Are there no Irish hearts that are moved by this thought? Surely the echo of GOD'S VOICE from Germany cannot find deafness in all Irish ears; and wherever it is heard, let not the evil enemy confuse the sound, by stirring up the din of ancient feuds in the Irish heart. There is no need to check this bursting effort after spiritual liberty, by imagining that the only way of escape is to join the ancient Protestants. England has had her own reformation, and failed in conveying it to Ireland; and now the days of THE IRISH REFORMATION may be come. Who will join in forming the IRISH CATHOLIC CHURCH, and in casting off that fatal clog, the usurped tyranny of the Bishop of Rome, which has hitherto kept it from being the Church of Christ indeed?

PRIESTS OF IRELAND! you know the secret workings of your consciences, and God knows them too. Which amongst you is the honest man that dares come forward, and fulfil in Ireland the important part that Czerski or that Ronge has acted in Germany? Which amongst you will recollect the movements of conscience within you, before it was entranced and Italianised, and will come forth, in the true cause of Christ and his Church, to find liberty of heart and soul yourselves, and to lead your flocks in that refreshing way of freedom, to the salvation that is in Christ alone?

May God in his great mercy carry these words with the power of HIS OWN VOICE to the hearts of multitudes of now enslaved Irishmen, and speedily raise up in his own way, by his own power, and with his own blessing, a goodly band to form THE CHRISTIAN CATHOLIC CHURCH OF IRELAND.

II.

A LOOK OUT OF IRELAND INTO GERMANY.

Who has ever climbed up Carran-tuel, and had the joy of throwing a look clean over Clare Island—that dot in the waters? Many a man of Kerry has done this, not satisfied with what he might see from the top of Tork, nor with a glimpse from the gap of Dunloe; he must reach the height of the Reeks to get to the very tip of all Ireland—the nearest step to the blessed blue heavens. When you get there, you may catch a sparkle from the sun, as it plays upon one of the three hundred and sixty-five lakes of Glengariff, you may peep over Skibbereen or Clonakilty; but there lie the green waters beyond, far, far away—so far that it wants a week's wind to blow a boat across them. It must be a sharp sight that sees even the waters from Carrantuel; but there is not a head in all Kerry with an eye that will see beyond them.

It is well for the priests that this is the case; for if the Irish could but see what is going on in the wide world, it would not be so easy a matter to keep the poor things in the dark, to suck their substance while the foot is on their necks. Oh, if some man of Kerry from the top of Carran-tuel could but have been looking on, and on, and on, about the month of August, in the year 1844, and had the power to distinguish the objects as his look went forward, what a wonderful story, and a true story, would he have told to his countrymen! Fancy such a look cast from that tip of all Ireland into Germany, and you shall hear what he might have seen.

There is a great town in Germany called Treves, and in it, amongst many churches, there is one greater than all the rest. Within the walls of this great church there is an ancient garment, and they say that it is the very coat without seam that was taken from our Lord Jesus Christ by his executioners when He was crucified. *They* say this; and why are people so mad as to venture upon such a story? The real coat without seam was cast lots for by heathen soldiers more than 1800 years ago, and fell to the lot of a poor godless wretch, since which it has never been heard of. But *they* say that this garment at Treves is the very coat; and they tell this lie upon very good authority—they have the authority of a Pope of Rome himself: and we have the authority of another Pope of Rome for saying that this is a lie; for the present man has solemnly declared that the real seamless coat is under the care of the priests in the great church of a town in France, called Argenteuil. Well, we will not stop to settle which of the two popes told the real lie; but the garment at Treves, which they pretend is able to do a great deal of good, must be one of those rags that the prophet Isaiah speaks of (chap. lxiv. 6).

But the man of Kerry, at the top of Carran-tuel, would tell you that he saw the Bishop of Treves and all his clergy consult together how they should get money for finishing another great cathedral; and they settled that they would bring out the old garment for a show, and tell the poor souls in Germany that every one of them would have a full and perfect absolution of all their sins, if they would make a pilgrimage to Treves to look at the Holy Coat, sincerely repenting of their sins, and doing penance for the same, or otherwise meaning to do so—provided, to be sure, that they contributed liberally towards the suitable endowment of the cathedral at Treves, etc.

The greater part of the people of Germany are under the power of the Romish priests, just in the same way as the folks are in Ireland; and the poor things are much in the same condition with respect to their worldly concerns too: thousands and thousands of people in Germany live upon no better fare, for them, than potatoes are for the Irish. But a Romish priest is a Romish priest all over the world; and the hearts and the cunning that can squeeze money out of the potatoe-eaters of Ireland, can manage the same matter out of the starving poor of Germany. It is all by making them believe the lies about purgatory, and the pope's power, and the charm of relics, and such like. And the poor things find it very hard to stand against what they tell them; only sometimes the priests push the falsehood so far, that it is harder to take in the lie than to resist the priests; and this is what has happened with the garment at Treves.

The coat with which the people were mocked at Treves, was shown in the cathedral from the 18th of August to the 6th of October, 1844, and the people from every parish were desired by the bishop to go to the cathedral in bodies on certain days, with their priests at their head. Every day it was station-day in all the parishes; and every poor soul that went on pilgrimage was sure to be washed clean of his sins, only he was to be careful to drop a suitable offering into the basin that was placed before the old coat. Before the six weeks were over, crowds upon crowds of Germans passed before this garment; and most of them had ruined themselves, that they might pay the coat for its kind service in saving them out of hell. The clergy counted the number of people, and tell us it was five hundred thousand. They counted the coin too, but they have not told us the number of pounds that they got—trust them for that.

Look out, man of Kerry, and tell us: can you see nothing else? were all the folks such fools as to worship the rag? Don't be so taken up with the beautiful sights, the flags and the banners, the flowers and the dresses of all these crowds of pilgrims. Don't give your ear only to the singing of the hymn that begins and ends with, "Holy Coat, pray for us." If the man of Kerry had looked right on, he might have seen in a little village a Romish priest writing a letter. He was no great man—no bishop; he did not live in a great town; but he was just a simple priest, who had got some common sense in his head, more kind feeling in his heart, and, it may be hoped, most of the Holy Ghost in his spirit. His name was John Ronge; and from his little village of Laura-hutte, he wrote on the 1st of October, 1844, a letter to all Christian people in Germany. It was a long one, but here are some parts of it:—

"Christian friends of the nineteenth century, you have heard —you know it, ye men of Germany—and you, ye German teachers of religion and learning, that what would once have sounded in our ears as mere fable and delusion, is neither fable nor delusion, but truth and certainty! Bishop Arnoldi, of Treves, has exhibited, as an object of religious contemplation and adoration, a garment designated the Coat of Christ!

"According to the last reports, no less than 500,000 persons have already made a pilgrimage to this relic; and thousands more are daily flocking thither, especially since the said vestment is pretended to have healed the sick, and performed other miracles. The fame of this is spreading throughout all lands, while, at the same time, French priests assert 'that they possess the genuine coat of Christ, and that the one at Treves is spurious.' Five hundred thousand individuals, five hundred thousand enlightened Germans, have already hastened to Treves, to behold and to worship a garment! The greater number of these hosts of pilgrims are of the very lowest classes of the people, living in the most abject poverty;

they have abandoned the cultivation of their fields, quitted their several employments, the care of their households, and the education of their children, to journey to an idol festival at Treves, to an unholy spectacle, which the Roman hierarchy displays before them. Yes; it is an idol festival, to which thousands of the credulous multitude are being enticed; and the feelings, the devotions which are due to God alone, are consecrated to a piece of cloth, the work of men's hands.

"And look at the pernicious results of these pilgrimages. Thousands deprive themselves of the necessaries of life to raise the money for their journey, and for the offerings which they have to present to the holy coat (offerings which the priests consume). This money is collected either by great personal deprivation, or by alms-begging; and on their return they must either starve and suffer need, or become enfeebled by sickness, in consequence of the fatigues and privations of the journey. . . .

"And the man who exhibits this garment, the work of human hands, to public view and adoration—who leads astray the religious feelings of the credulous, the ignorant, or the suffering—who thus gives an impetus to superstition and vice—who artfully extorts their money and their substance from a poor and starving population—who holds up the German people to the derision of other nations—and who attracts the dark and lowering thunderclouds which hang suspended over our heads into a yet denser mass—this man is a Bishop—a German Bishop. It is Arnoldi, Bishop of Treves!

"Bishop Arnoldi, of Treves, I turn to you. . . . Do you not know—as Bishop you ought to know—that the founder of the Christian religion bequeathed to his disciples and his followers, not his coat, but his Spirit?' His coat, Bishop Arnoldi, of Treves, fell to the lot of his executioners! Do you not know—as Bishop you ought to know—that Christ taught—' God is a Spirit; and they that worship Him must worship Him in Spirit and in truth'? And He may be worshipped everywhere, not only in the Temple at Jerusalem, on Mount Gerizim, or at Treves, before the holy coat. Do you not know—as Bishop you ought to know—that the Gospel expressly forbids the worship of every image and of every relic? And that the Christians in the Apostolic age, and during the first three centuries, tolerated neither image nor relics in their churches, though they might have obtained them in abundance. . . .

". . . . Bishop Arnoldi, of Treves, you know all this, and far better, doubtless, than I can tell you; you also know the consequences which superstition and the idolatrous worship of relics have wrought among us—the political and spiritual thraldom of Germany; and yet you set up your relic for public adoration! And were it even possible that you did not know all this, that your only aim in exhibiting this relic were the weal of Christendom, you have nevertheless burdened your conscience with a twofold sin, from which you cannot clear yourself. In the first place, it is unpardonable, if the said vestment really possess healing virtue, that you have withheld the boon from suffering humanity till the year 1844, and in the second place, it is unpardonable that you have taken offerings of money from these hundred thousands of pilgrims. Is it not unpardonable that you, as Bishop, should take money from the starving poor of our nation? And the more so since only a few weeks ago you yourself beheld hundreds, impelled by famine and distress, driven into rebellion, despair, and death. Do not suffer yourself to be deceived by the throng of thousands upon thousands, but believe me, that while hundreds of thousands of Germans repair full of fervour to Treves, millions are, like myself, filled with profound abhorrence and holy indignation at your scandalous exhibition.

"This indignation prevails not only among individual ranks or parties, but among all classes; nay, even among the Roman Catholic priesthood. Judgment will overtake you sooner than you are aware, Arnoldi! . . .

"And you, fellow-countrymen, whether you dwell near or at a distance from Treves, unite your efforts to prevent the stigma from resting any longer upon the German name. You have magistrates, wardens, and provincial diets and assemblies; work through their medium. It is high time that each and all resolve to make a bold stand, and with their utmost energy to oppose and restrain the tyrannical power of the Roman hierarchy. For it is not at Treves alone that this modern absurdity of traffic in indulgences is carried on; you well know that in the east, and the west, the north, and the south, rosary, mass, absolution, burial-monies, and the like, are every day collected; and that the night of spiritual gloom grows darker and darker. . . .

"Finally; you, my dear brethren in the ministry, whose sole aims and wishes centre in the welfare of your flocks, the honour, liberty, and happiness of your country, keep no longer silence. You sin against religion, against your native land, against your holy calling, if you longer hesitate to give effect to your better convictions. Prove yourselves to be the true disciples of Him who sacrificed all for Truth, Light, and Liberty; prove that you have inherited, not his coat, but his Spirit.

"JOHANNES RONGE."

Could any Irishman read this letter without crying out to the man of Kerry at the top of Carran-tuel—" Tell us, what do you see next? Go on now, if you please, and inform us what followed."

What was like to follow to the man that wrote it? Wouldn't he have been cursed by bell, book, and candle, if it had been in old Ireland? Curses grow at Rome, and are sent over all the Pope's countries, to one place as well as another; so his slaves in Germany get the same treatment as his slaves in Erin. Priest Ronge was degraded and excommunicated; and as much cut off from heaven as a Pope can do it; but as that's none at all, heaven is as open to Ronge now as the Lord Jesus Christ has made it. But the letter went about all Germany, in spite of the excommunication. In one city (Leipsic) 50,000 copies of it were sold in a fortnight; and in every city the people could talk of nothing else. Why was this? Each thought he heard his own voice when it was read to him—each felt that it told the thoughts of his own mind, and the feelings of his own heart. Who has not had a secret on his mind that he did not dare tell to anybody, but has jumped for joy when another has spoken it out? and then he too gets heart to speak what is in him, and let out his feelings and not be afraid. So it was in Germany—hundreds and hundreds of Roman Catholics took courage, and told each other how ashamed they were at being slaves to the Roman Bishop. Yes, thousands have taken courage, and vowed that, for Christ's sake, and for the honour of his truth, they will be such slaves no longer.

Was not this the work of God? Take one token that it was so, out of many. If the man of Kerry had looked a little more·

to the north, he might have seen far away in another part of Germany, another priest in the small town of Schneidemuhl. There God had been preparing a little flock by the pious teaching of John Czerski, a Catholic priest, whose heart had been touched by the Spirit of truth, and who was gradually getting rid of the chains that bound him to the Roman Bishop. When the scandalous pilgrimage to worship the old coat at Treves was going on, the hearts at Schneidemuhl could bear the shame no longer; and Czerski came forward, solemnly and strongly to protest against the tyranny and deceit of Rome. God had provided the instruments in different parts, to call upon the Germans to turn from the lying devices of the Pope; and so the voice ran along all Germany, from one end of it to the other, and the cry set up by Ronge, and that by Czerski, joined into a song of harmony, and the chorus was echoed in shouts from German hearts—" We will cast off false Rome," was the song which followed the hymn—" Holy Coat, pray for us."

It was not long before the people in every place gathered together quietly, and found that the curse of the priests was only an empty sound that did no harm; and they found, too, that the blessing of God was with them to keep them from harm, and to lead them to good. They did not want to cast off God's religion, but rather to cast off all the new inventions man had tacked to it:—it was not the power of God that they resisted, but that evil power which kept them from God in Christ—it was not the Catholic character that they gave up, but they threw off with courage the foreign Roman yoke. In various towns, the children of religious freedom arranged their several declarations of the faith in Christ Jesus; and no wonder that at such a moment, and under such a feeling, many different bodies of Christians did this without much consideration, or agreement one with another. A few months, however, was enough to remedy this; and the Catholic Christians of various towns sent deputies to meet together, and arrange a confession of faith, which they could all agree to, as the truth in Christ Jesus—the only truth given to man from heaven. And in acknowledging this truth, they call themselves the German Catholic Church of Christ. Those who form this Catholic Church stand out from their old tyrants. They do but step aside, and cease to fear them, and they find to their surprise and joy that there is no need to fear them; and that all the power of the priests rested upon their own slavish obedience. Whole congregations have turned from the priests; and though the priests excommunicate them all, yet they all communicate together, and so they excommunicate the priests. At the present time, there are, however, twenty-six priests who have left Rome, and joined Ronge and Czerski, and helped to arrange the German Catholic Church; and this Church is now formed in one hundred and ninety-three different towns and places in Germany.

The articles of faith which these Catholics have adopted is the same in substance as the ancient Christians held from the time of our Lord Himself, and can be proved from the Word of God. In contrast from the Romish Church they maintain, amongst others, the following points:—

1. They maintain that every man has a right to read the Book of God for himself; and they refuse to believe what is told them about the other world, or the way to be saved, unless they can see for themselves that it can be proved out of that blessed Book.

2. They will not allow the worship offered up to God to be spoken in a language which the people do not understand.

3. They refuse to pray to dead men and women; or to believe that their bones, and the things that belonged to them while living, have any power to heal or to help.

4. They deny that Christians are called upon to acknowledge the Bishop of Rome as having any power from St. Peter, or any peculiar authority from Christ; and they refuse to acknowledge themselves bound to obey him or his agents.

5. They maintain that no man has power, by a word or touch, to turn either bread or wine into the "whole body, blood, soul, and divinity of the Lord Jesus Christ;" and they claim the right of the laity to partake of both the bread and the wine in

the Sacrament of the Lord's Supper, as well as those who administer that holy ordinance.

6. They maintain that the clergy have no right to require the people to confess to them, before they will give them the Lord's Supper.

7. They maintain that marriage is honourable, and holy, and good, for all classes of persons; and that the clergy may and ought to marry as well as the people.

Oh! if there were no waters between the Shannon and the Rhine, there would be no need to give a man of Kerry a spyglass, and send him to the top of Carran-tuel, to bring his countrymen an account of all this; for surely the report of it must have found its way along the villages that would then cover the ground that the waves wash now; and spite of priest or Pope, the poor Irish Romans would then get a chance of tasting something of the liberty wherewith Christ makes souls free, in the place of the bondage with which the Pope makes souls slaves. Even the poor fellows that make a yearly pilgrimage to gather the harvests of other nations might then have lengthened their long journey, and gathered in Germany a harvest of God's truth for themselves, and stored it up and brought it home for their wives and their children. What might be expected to have happened in such a case as that? Let us gather from the knowledge of what has really happened in Germany, what might then be taking place in dear old Ireland.

The news would arrive in some little town in Ireland that thousands upon thousands of Roman Catholic Germans had declared themselves Catholic without being Roman—had left their priests in a body, and found that the priests could do them no harm for it—had dared, one and all, to read God's Book, in spite of the priests forbidding them. Then many an Irishman that heard it would take courage, and talk freely and boldly to his Catholic neighbour; and if some among the better scholars and upper people did this, they would feel it to be a time for stepping forward to help their brothers, and would venture to take a little more upon themselves than in common times they would like to do. And many a company of the poorer ones would agree together to go to some of the upper sort, and call upon them to come forward and help them. Then remembering that the priests are men and brothers too, whose hearts can be touched by the power of the same God, who has all hearts at his command, all the wise and awakened Catholics in the place would go together to the priest of the place—be he Curate, or Vicar-General, or the Bishop himself, and they would tell him that they were determined, from that moment, to be true Christian Catholics; and that they began to be so by leaving the communion of Rome, and by being in communion amongst themselves as Irish, not Roman, Catholics. Then they would invite the priest to join them, and bid him give a proof that he did so by at once reading the Bible to them, and saying Mass in their own tongue instead of Latin; and by administering to some proper persons amongst them the wine of the Holy Communion, as well as the bread.

The priest would either follow the example of Ronge, and agree to join the people, or he would refuse. If he agreed, then the people would rejoice, and hail him as one appointed by God to help in directing them right, instead of leading them in the wrong way as of old. They would choose out three or four, or half a dozen of their lay brothers in whom they had confidence, and they would appoint them as the Care-takers to watch for the ordering which God's providence might make necessary— they would bid these take counsel with the fatherly pastor whom the goodness of God had provided for them by turning the heart of the priest; and then leaving the matter for the present in these hands, they would wait a while in prayer and patience, till new events called them to maintain their new position of freedom.

But if the priest should refuse to join the people, or to separate himself from the tyrant system of the Pope of Rome, then would come the test of courage and of confidence in God. It is written in the book of God concerning Rome, "And I heard another **VOICE FROM HEAVEN**, saying, **COME OUT OF HER, MY PEOPLE**, that ye be not partakers of her sins, and that ye receive not of her plagues" (Rev. xviii. 4); and the time to which that voice from heaven referred is now nigh at hand. Christians dare not let the refusal of a Popish priest make them refuse to obey the voice of God. The Spirit that would move the people in any parish in Ireland to go so far as to ask the priest to join them in leaving Rome, would move them on, though they were forced to leave their priest behind them, after giving him a chance of getting free along with themselves.

Then the people would choose out half a dozen, it may be, of the fittest and the wisest men amongst them, and just put the management of the future concerns of the Irish Catholic Church into their hands, and keep quiet at home in constant earnest prayer that the Lord would mercifully bless all their deliberations; and what the half dozen Care-takers decided for the course of conduct for the whole, that would each member willingly consent to.

But what course *would* the company of Care-takers pursue? The course may be difficult, but not doubtful. They would first select a proper person to act *for the present* as LEADER IN PRAYER, and they would provide for him the best-written prayers they can procure in their own tongue, to suit the feelings of the people; and they would call the people together twice on every Sunday to join in these prayers, and to hear the Book of God read by the leader; and they would commend the head of every family who can read to make use of some of the same prayers, and of the same blessed book, every day in their own houses, in company with some of their neighbours. This arrangement could be only for a time, not to leave the Christian Catholics without the means of approaching God unitedly, at a period when God's presence amongst them was more than commonly required.

But having attended to this pressing want, the company of Care-takers would lose no time in consulting with their fellow-Catholics in the next parish, and in the neighbouring towns far and near; and as the news would have spread to one as well as another parish, God's work would appear in one as well as in another; and so in many places many hearts would be moved, and that which might be wanting through the ignorance of one band of Irish Catholics would be supplied through the wisdom of another; and deputies from each little band would appoint a place and time to meet, and they would compare their circumstances and condition, and put the whole together to find the wisest way to act; and they would pray to God to direct them, and many Christian hearts would be praying for them, and it would be a one-hearted body this Irish Catholic Church. May He that is above all bless it!

Is there any Irishman that reads this who wants to know what next would be done in such a case? The news which would have been brought over to Ireland before now, if no sea separated it from Germany, has been longer delayed to be sure, but it has come at last, and the Irishman who reads this has heard the blessed sound; and if it is he that wants to know what would come next, let him and his Catholic neighbours set to work at once to get on as far as has been supposed already; and when he has come so far, then he himself shall be the man to tell us what will come next. Only one thing is sure, that the work that is begun for the glory of God and the freedom of souls is certain to be blessed in the end, through whatever difficulties and sufferings the Lord may see fit to bring us to the reward.

The following is the tract referred to in Chapter VII.:—

III.

IRISHMEN'S RIGHTS.

EVERY man has got his own RIGHTS, except the man that lets them be taken away from him; and it would not be hard to say what the like of such a man is, only that it is not civil to call names. Yet to have some rights, and not to know what they are, is as good as not having them at all; so I will tell you what some of an Irishman's rights are.

Every man has a right to breathe the free air of heaven at least; and will any one deny that a man has a right to the springs of water from the earth? Who has ever been thirsty on a warm day, and felt the freshening of a good draught from the river as it flows along? Has not every man a right to that? Now, if you will attend to a story, you shall see what all this is driving at.

It was on a hot day in August—suppose we call it the twenty-fourth: that was a very hot day once upon a time—some Irish boys were working hard in a dry part of the land where there was no water. The Shannon flowed not far from them, and when they were all dried up with thirst, off they set to quench it at those waters. But they were stopped short of the banks of the river, for the only part they could come at was fenced off with a railing, made of strong posts, very high, with spikes at the top, and a deep ditch to hinder coming near. The poor fellows could see through it to be sure, so that they could observe that the river was broad, and shone beautifully as it rolled along. There was a gate to this fence, and a priest stood inside to take care of it; but it was bolted and barred, so that nobody could get through to get at the waters of the river.

"Please your reverence," said one of the boys, "we want a drop of water; sure every Irishman has a right to a sup of the Shannon."

"Never think of such a thing," said his reverence, "you are much better without it; it is dirty water, and won't do you any good."

"Dirty or clean, please your reverence, it will save a man's tongue from burning, and the boys are all dying with drought."

"Och," cries another, "look just over the river, there are plenty of them drinking of the waters on the other side." And so sure enough there were.

"You are mistaken," said his reverence, "those are nothing but Sasenachs; such water is only fit for heretics."

"But is a poor Irish Roman to perish for thirst, then," says

Pat, "and the river all flowing before him, enough to make his mouth water, if it was all dried up past watering?"

Hard as they all tried, his reverence would not open the way to the river.

"Is his reverence never thirsty himself," cried Mick, "that he has no compassion upon the throats of his flock?"

"And don't you know, Mick, that his reverence does not trouble the water when he is thirsty, seeing that he has got a regular supply of the real whiskey that has passed the exciseman, besides the occasional drops of potteen? and these last are none of the fewest."

Now, who shall deny that these poor fellows had a right to a drink of the Shannon, all large, and broad, and deep as it is, so that all the throats in Ireland would never make the sea think it was less of a river, when she kissed its broad mouth between Kerry and Clare? And yet these poor fellows were not the more like to get their right. But presently there was some one seen inside the railings, that would be trying to help the boys in their extremity of thirst. Nobody could tell how he got there, whether he scrambled over the fence, or swam from the other side, or more likely dropped down from heaven, sent by the holy and blessed Lord Himself. He ran to the river, and dipping his hand in, he brought as much as he could in the hollow of it, and the best of good water it was, and he just handed it over to the first poor fellow that would take it; but the priest ran to stop him, and then he slipped round to the other end with another handful of clear water; and so he slipped about whilst the priest was in a terrible passion—mad entirely. But some of the poor fellows got a sprinkling, and they that did found it so refreshing that nothing would serve them but they must have some more; and so they went higher up or lower down the river, however far it might be, and never rested till they came to the place where they could stoop down and drink, and drink, and drink, so that they never thirsted again (John iv. 13, 14); while the poor fellows that stopped outside the priest's railings were left to die; for "never mind," said the priest, "I'll say a Mass for their souls when they are in purgatory, and that will be better than a drop of water to save their lives now."

I was going to give an explanation of this story, but there is no occasion; for is there ever an Irishman that wants to be told what it means? and why should I waste time to tell him the meaning when surely it's in his heart, he feels what it means? And is it not the Lord Jesus Christ Himself, blessed be his holy name, who has said, "If any man thirst, let him come to Me and drink"? (John vii. 37.) Every man has a right to "take the water of life freely." This is so plain and so certain, that the Church of Rome itself does not pretend to deny it; only it sets the priests to watch the gate, and bids them take care who they let in. Now it is the priests who keep the gate barred, and refuse to let a man in at all; they will not let the people read the Bible because it contains some such words as these, "Woe to you Scribes and Pharisees, hypocrites, because you shut the kingdom of heaven against men, for you yourselves do not enter in, and those that are going in you suffer not to enter" (Matt. xxiii. 13).

The fact is that the priests are required by the Church of Rome to know the Scriptures themselves, that they may be able to judge to whom they may give permission to read the Book of God. Every man has a right to read the Bible; it is the right of his soul, given him by God, as much as it is the right of his body to breathe the air of heaven, or drink the waters of the earth, given him by God; and it is the height of wickedness that any hindrance should be placed in the way of a man when he is thirsty for his right. But if people will be so foolish as to allow themselves to be hindered from drinking freely, when the river of God's Word is flowing before their eyes, then at least let Irish Roman Catholics understand that their own Church acknowledges the right of every man to go to his priest, to ask him to read the Bible himself, that he may see what part the people may read.

Your priest has lately had a friendly letter sent to him, respectfully reminding his reverence of his duty to read the Bible himself. Perhaps you would like to see this letter, so a copy of it is sent to you, and you will find from this that, according to the rules of the Church of Rome, anybody may read the Book of God if he has got a permission under the hand of a priest; and in case you would like to have such a permission, you may make use of that which is sent to you with this, and in which a true priest gives you the free liberty to write your own or any other name in the blank that is left for it.

You are advised to begin to act upon this permission at once; but for fear you may be standing thirsty outside the paling, the man dropped from heaven in the inside runs to you with a handful of the water of life; and though it is but a drop, he sends it you in earnest prayer that it may refresh your soul with a blessing. This drop of the precious water comes to you in the shape of some small portions of the Book of God. Take care how you receive these NOW, for by the welcome you give them you will be judged by God, and there may come a time when you may be like the man in the parable, who said, "Send Lazarus, that he may dip the tip of his finger in water to cool my tongue, for I am tormented in this flame" (Luke xvi. 24); and know that there may be something even in this drop of the water of life now, which God, in his mercy, may make the means of saving you from that torment HEREAFTER.

THE PERMISSION BY AUTHORITY.

This is to certify, that the BLESSED LORD HIMSELF gives you, Mr. ——— full and free permission and commandment to "search the Scriptures" (John v. 39), in the language you understand; and I would advise you as a friend, lest the LORD should judge you and punish you for neglect of his Word, to take the Bible, and search it, and to try if I am telling you the truth, for HE has laid it upon me to send this permission to you. I am, your friend, and

A TRUE PRIEST.

THE DROP OF THE WATER OF LIFE.

Referred to in "Irishmen's Rights."

IF THE SON SHALL MAKE YOU FREE, YE SHALL BE FREE INDEED.—John viii. 36.

YE SHALL KNOW THE TRUTH, AND THE TRUTH SHALL MAKE YOU FREE.—John viii. 12.

God so loved the world as to give his only-begotten Son, that whosoever *believeth in Him may not perish*, but may have everlasting life."—John iii. 16.

A faithful saying, and worthy of all acceptation, that Christ Jesus came into the world to *save sinners.*—1 Tim. i. 15.

The *blood* of *Jesus Christ* his Son *cleanseth us from all sin.*—1 John i. 7.

Believe in the Lord Jesus Christ, and *thou* shalt be *saved.*—Acts xvi. 31.

There is one God, and *one Mediator* between God and men, the *man Christ Jesus.*—1 Tim. ii. 5.

Come unto *Me*, all ye that *labour* and are burthened, and I will refresh you.—Matt. xi. 28.

I, even I, am He that *blotteth* out thy transgressions for mine *own sake*, and will not remember *thy* sins.—Isa. xliii. 25.

Call upon *Me* in the day of trouble: I will deliver thee, and thou shalt glorify *Me.*—Ps. l. 15.

Ask, and it shall be given you; seek, and ye shall find; knock, and it shall be opened unto you. . . . If ye then, being evil, know how to give good gifts unto your children: how much more shall your Father from heaven give the *good Spirit* to them that ask Him.—Luke xi. 9, 13.

I said, I will *confess* my transgressions *unto the Lord;* and *Thou* forgavest the iniquity of my sin.—Ps. xxxii. 5.

Ho, every one that thirsteth, come ye to the waters, and he that hath no money; come ye, buy, and eat; yea, come, buy wine and milk *without money and without price.*—Isa. lv. 1.

He that *rejecteth Me*, and *receiveth not my words*, hath one that judgeth him: *the word that I have spoken*, the same shall judge him in *the last day.*—John xii. 48.

COPY OF THE LETTER SENT TO THE PRIEST.
Referred to in " Irishmen's Rights."

REVEREND SIR,—You are respectfully requested to give serious consideration to the following argument, concerning which your practical opinion may shortly be called for.

You are no doubt aware, that it is by a mistake that the Protestants assert, that the reading of the Bible is absolutely prohibited by the Roman Catholic doctrines.

You are also aware, that the true state of the case is, that the laity are forbidden to read any version of the Holy Scriptures, without ecclesiastical authority first had and obtained in the form of a written permission from the priest.

The priest is thus constituted the judge of the propriety of granting such permission in each particular case, and of conceding to any individual of his flock such license to read the Holy Scriptures in whole or in part, as to him may seem right. While, therefore, the reading of the Scriptures by the laity is restrained and limited, not only is no restraint or limit imposed upon the priest, as regards his own reading of the Bible, but it is distinctly required of each priest that he should make himself acquainted with the Holy Scriptures, in order to be able to form a judgment, whether they may be safely read, in whole or in part, by any individual of his flock who may apply to him for such a permission as he is authorized to grant.

It being thus plainly the duty of every priest of the Roman Catholic Church to read the Holy Scriptures himself, you are respectfully asked—Have *you* read the Holy Scriptures?

If not the whole, have you at least read the New Testament?

Have you read it in the original Greek? or, should this be difficult to you, have you read the Latin vulgate?

Have you made yourself acquainted with the versions in

English and in Irish, which are those likely to be found in the hands of your flock?

If this should not be the case, it is respectfully suggested to you, that you should apply yourself to such reading at once; or how could you be capable of forming a judgment, in case any of your flock should exercise this undoubted right of asking your permission to read the Scriptures, upon such reasonable grounds as no honest man ought to refuse to consider?

Suppose a dozen or twenty respectable Roman Catholics, such as farmers, or tradesmen, or gentlemen, living in your parish, were to ask such a permission from you, what reason could you give for refusing, if you had never read the Scriptures yourself? It is by no means unlikely that such an application may be made to you by even a greater number than a dozen or twenty.

In case you have any difficulty in getting a copy of the Scriptures to begin at once, the following short extracts are taken from the Douay New Testament.

EXTRACTS.

O foolish, and slow of heart to believe in all things which the prophets have spoken. Ought not Christ to have suffered these things, and so to enter into his glory? And beginning at Moses and all the prophets, He expounded to them in all the Scriptures, the things that were concerning Him.—Luke xxiv. 25—27.

Search the Scriptures, for you think in them to have life everlasting; and the same are they that give testimony of Me. —John v. 39.

He that despiseth Me, and receiveth not my words, hath one that judgeth him; the word that I have spoken, the same shall judge him in the last day.—John xii. 48.

Now this is eternal life: That they may know Thee, the only true God, and Jesus Christ, whom Thou hast sent.—John xvii. 3.

Now these were more noble than those in Thessalonica, who

received the Word with all eagerness, daily searching the Scriptures, whether these things were so.—Acts xvii. 11.

For what things soever were written, were written for our learning: that through patience and comfort of the Scriptures, we might have hope.—Rom. xv. 4.

A faithful saying: if a man desire the office of a bishop, he desireth a good work. It behoveth therefore a bishop to be blameless, the husband of one wife, sober, prudent, of good behaviour, chaste, given to hospitality, a teacher, not given to wine, no striker, but modest, not quarrelsome, not covetous, but one that ruleth well his own house, having his children in subjection with all chastity. But if a man know not how to rule his own house, how shall he take care of the Church of God.—1 Tim. iii. 1—5.

Now the Spirit manifestly saith, that in the last times some shall depart from the faith, giving heed to spirits of error, and doctrines of devils, speaking lies in hypocrisy, and having their conscience seared, forbidding to marry, to abstain from meats, which God hath created to be received with thanksgiving by the faithful, and by them that have known the truth.—1 Tim. iv. 1—3.

For the Word of God is living and effectual, and more piercing than any two-edged sword; and reaching unto the division of the soul and the spirit, of the joints also and the marrow, and is a discerner of the thoughts and intents of the heart.—Heb. iv. 12.

The following is the tract referred to in Chapter VIII.:—

IV.
THE FOOD OF MAN.

"WHAT sort of food have you got in Ireland? and how much of it?"

"Sure the food of man has failed altogether—there is not a

potatoe of the right sort to be found from Athlone to the sea;—and what will we do it's Him that's wiser than the wisest among us that must tell. You may dig a whole ridge, and not get a pot-full, and when the mother has cut out a few bits from some things that are ashamed to call themselves potatoes, and has left more outsides than in—it's the pig herself that takes to being genteel, that would not taste them at all—let alone the little family. Over the starving to death, there'll be no paying the rent that's due this year, nor any other dues; unless the dues of them that know how to squeeze the marrow out of a dry bone."

"Who do you mean by that?"

"Is it your honour that asks, with a tongue that won't let your teeth forget that they grew in Connaught? Haven't you found out that the Priests feed, let who will famish?"

"But how is it that the food of man is blighted entirely? What has been the cause?"

"It's the truth that your honour speaks there—it is the food of man that's blighted, and none other—the weakest weed by the side of the black stalk of the potatoe blossoms as elegant as if it was laughing at the boys that got nothing but weeds for their labour. The blessing of St Patrick has clean gone out of the land—the Almighty has sent us a judgment—the blessed mother of God has not had Hail Maries enough;—yet if they all handled their beads like that creature of mine, sure the Holy Virgin should not be in want of Hail Maries. There is a curse on the food of man."

"Of man, my friend! what do you mean by that? what is man?"

"I don't receive your honour's meaning."

"Do you know what a *man* is? what *you* are?"

"I'm an Irishman, please your honour."

"Put out your hand—is that *you*? or your foot?"

"Tom O'Creagh got his arm smashed under a waggon, and drives his car with a stump!—and Dan Flaherty has got a wooden leg."

"Then neither the hand nor the foot can be the man—nor

the tongue, nor any other part of the body. Were you at the funeral of Michael O'Sullivan last week?"

"It was myself kenned the loudest cry at the wake."

"And where was Michael all the while? he wasn't in the coffin, for that was only the corpse—where was the man Michael?"

"By father Meghan's story to the widow, Mick was in Purgatory: for when she had sold his clothes and the spade, she had to borrow five shillings to make up the money for father Meghan to say Masses to help him a bit."

"Wherever he was or is now, you see, my friend, that his body was not himself. It's himself that's gone out of the body, and the body is crumbling to dust. It's yourself that's in your body—that makes your body alive. You and your body are two different things;—and it's *the man* that makes the body of any importance—the body wants food because the man is in it—and the man must live when he leaves the body—wherever he goes to, he is alive. Now the man within the body—that is, the precious soul—has to be fed; the body craves food only because there is a man's soul in it, which wants its proper food, that it may live in the presence of God for ever and ever."

"And can your honour tell us what's the food that is proper for that?"

"God Himself has told us. He says in his blessed book—

'Agur do ḟreagair Íosa é, ag rád Atá rgríobtha, Ná leḃ haráng a ṁáing maṁṡroṡ an duṁne, aċd leḃ gaċ nḋle ḃréiṫir Dé.'

This is in the tongue of our dear land;—the Douay version, as acknowledged by the Roman Catholic bishops, puts this English on it:—

'And Jesus answered him, It is written that man liveth not by bread alone, but by every word of God.'—St. Luke, chap. iv., verse 4.

"So you see, my friend, that it is a clear and certain truth, acknowledged by all, that while the body is kept alive by bread and the fruits of the earth, the soul (which is the only thing that makes the body of any value) is kept in a state of life by 'every word of God.'"

"I think I see your honour's meaning—but this Word of God—this food for the man inside us—we have not got it at all at all."

"Is not there Batt. Flanagan that's willing to teach any man to read the Word of God in old Irish; and will read it by the hour together to any that will go to hear?"

"Aye, but your honour must know that the priest has cursed Batt. Flanagan with bell, book, and candle from the altar. Myself heard the bell, and saw him close the book, and quench the candle; and his reverence threatened to do the same on any that would learn of him, or hear him read; he said the Bible was the devil's book, and taught the way to hell."

"Did you not tell me just now that there was a curse upon the food of man? You meant the potatoes—and so there is. But who began the cursing? 'Man liveth not by bread alone, but by every word of God.' Your hand, and your foot, and your tongue, are kept alive by potatoes; but all those are only the instruments of your soul—and your soul is kept alive by the Word of God—that is the food of man—really *the man*. The poor souls in Ireland have been kept in a starving state, unfit for God or for heaven, because men have dared to curse the food of man's soul—the blessed Word of God—and God has had long patience; but the cursings have grown louder, and stronger, and more daring, and at last God has answered the cursings of the food mercifully provided for man's soul, by withholding his blessing from the land, so that it will not yield the food for man's body. One blast of God's breath brings a real curse on the land; but the daring curse of the priest is but the breath of a man that can do nothing. Oh foolish people to be kept from the food by which your soul can live for ever, by the idle and blasphemous breath of a man. Oh foolish people to make it needful that God should undeceive you by sending a real curse upon the food by which your bodies are supported.

"In order to remove this anger of God from you, hasten to

say to your priests, we will have the Word of God, which is the real food of man; for 'it is written, MAN LIVETH NOT BY BREAD ALONE, BUT BY EVERY WORD OF GOD.'"

QUESTION.

Why do the priests strive to hinder the people from learning to read the Word of God (the food of man's soul) in the language they can best understand and feel?

ANSWERS.

Because—The priests perform worship in the Latin, which, to the people of Ireland, is an unknown tongue. But in the Word of God it is written, "Except you utter by the tongue plain speech, how shall it be known what is said? For you shall be speaking into the air. There are, for example, so many kinds of tongues in this world; and none is without voice. If then I know not the power of the voice, I shall be to him to whom I speak a barbarian; and he that speaketh, a barbarian to me." —1st to the Cor. xiv. 9—18.

Because—The priests teach that the bread and wine in the Lord's Supper are the very "body, blood, soul, and divinity of our Lord Jesus Christ." But in the Word of God it is written, "that the Lord Jesus, the same night in which He was betrayed, took bread, and giving thanks, broke, and said: Take ye, and eat: this is my body, which shall be delivered for you; this do for the commemoration of Me. In like manner also the chalice, after He had supped, saying: This chalice is the New Testament in my blood; this do ye, as often as you shall drink, for the commemoration of Me. For as often as you shall eat this bread, and drink the chalice, you shall show the death of the Lord until He come."—1st to the Cor. xi. 23—26. No one *reading this* would suppose that when the Lord Himself gave to his disciples with his own hand, before his body was broken, or his blood shed, could be the very body which was giving it; but it would be easy to see that the Lord meant the bread and the chalice to be symbols, one of his body, the other of "the New Testament in his blood." The apostle also calls the bread, bread four times, when speaking of it after consecration.

Because—The priests say that in their constant repetition of the sacrifice of the Mass, Jesus Christ is always in the midst of us with his corporeal presence. But in the Word of God it is written, that our Lord said, when speaking of his body, upon which ointment had been poured, "the poor you have always with you: but Me you have not always."—St. Matt. xxvi. 11.

Because—The priests teach for doctrines the commandments of men; but in the Word of God it is written, "In vain do they worship Me, teaching doctrines and commandments of men."—St. Matt. xv. 9.

Because—The priests teach that there are many persons who act as mediators between God and men—such as the Virgin Mary, St. Joseph, etc., etc. But in the Word of God it is written, "There is one God, and one Mediator of God and men, the man Christ Jesus."—1st Tim. ii. 5.

Because—The priests teach that there is a place which they call Purgatory, where souls go to be cleansed from certain sins, beside the application of the atonement of Christ. But in the Word of God no mention is made of any such place; but it is written on the contrary, that "the blood of Jesus Christ his Son cleanseth us from all sin."—1st of St. John i. 7.

Here are some of the causes why the priests hinder the people from learning to read the Scriptures; and any man who uses the right to obtain the food of his soul, and learns to read "every word of God" in spite of the priests, will soon find out a great many more such causes. All the quotations are made from their own Douay version, which is authorized by the Roman Catholic bishops.

V.

THE following was the "Constitution of the Society," together with its "Object and Rules," as they were approved at the First Meeting of the Society. The names of all the original Officers are added:—

CONSTITUTION OF THE SOCIETY.

I.—The Society shall be called "The Society for Irish Church Missions to the Roman Catholics," and shall be under the direction of a President and Vice-Presidents, a Treasurer, a Committee, and Secretaries, all being Members of the United Church of England and Ireland.

II.—Annual Subscribers of One Guinea and upwards (if Clergymen, Half-a-Guinea), and Collectors of Fifty-two Shillings and upwards per Annum, shall be Members of the Society during the continuance of such Subscriptions or Collections. Benefactors of Ten Guineas and upwards, Clergymen making Congregational Collections to the amount of Twenty Guineas, and Executors paying to the amount of Fifty Pounds, shall be Members for Life. The Committee shall have the power of appointing such persons as have rendered essential services to the Society Honorary Members for Life.

III.—The Committee shall consist of a number not exceeding twenty-four Lay-Members of the United Church, and of all Clergymen who may be Members of the Society. The President, Vice-Presidents, Treasurer, and Secretaries, shall be considered *ex officio* Members of the Committee.

IV.—The Committee shall meet at such time and place as they may appoint; their meetings always to be opened with prayer. Five Members shall be a quorum.

V.—The Committee shall have power to appoint such Officers and Assistants, and to make such Regulations, as they shall deem necessary for the well-conducting of the affairs of the Society.

VI.—An Annual Meeting of the Members of the Society shall be held in London, when the proceedings of the foregoing year shall be reported, the Accounts be presented, and a Treasurer and Committee chosen.

VII.—None of the Rules of the Institution shall be repealed or altered, nor any new ones established, but at the Annual Meeting, or at a Special Meeting called for that purpose.

VIII.—Three Auditors shall be appointed by the Committee annually, for the purpose of auditing the accounts of the Society.

THE OBJECT AND RULES OF THE SOCIETY.

THE great Object of the Society shall be to promote Church Missions to the Roman Catholics of Ireland through the Established Church in Ireland; the chief attention being directed to the English-speaking population, except in the Missions in Galway, and except in such districts as may not be occupied by the Irish Society; and this object shall be carried on with cordial goodwill to the Irish Society, labouring in their important sphere among the Irish-speaking population.

In pursuing this object, the Committee will adopt the following Regulations:—

I.—At the request of Incumbents, they will aid in supporting Assistant-Ministers in parishes containing a large Roman Catholic population. The nomination and appointment of these Ministers to be subject to Rule VII., being similar to that of the Church Pastoral Aid Society, with the understanding, that ministration to the Roman Catholics shall be their distinct and peculiar object.

II.—Assistant-Ministers may also be appointed, under the direction of the Bishop, for the Roman Catholics of a whole diocese.

III.—In parishes where the Incumbent would be favourable to such efforts, the temporary services of able and experienced Clergymen may be engaged, in visiting districts, in giving lectures, and in preaching to the Roman Catholics.

IV.—Courses of Lectures, by competent Lecturers, on the great subjects in controversy between the Churches of England and Rome, will be encouraged and upheld in the principal towns in Ireland.

V.—The Committee to be at liberty, according to its resources, to adopt any measures that may tend to the furtherance of the conversion of the Roman Catholic population of Ireand, by means consistent with the principles of the United Church of England and Ireland; and to maintain friendly communication with all Church of England Societies seeking the spiritual welfare of Ireland.

VI.—The Committee will gladly be the medium of sending any aid which contributors may wish to appropriate to the Religious Societies they have already assisted; and a friendly intercourse shall be maintained with other Protestants engaged in the same benevolent design of communicating the Gospel of Jesus Christ to the Roman Catholics of Ireland.

VII.—No grant from the Society's Funds for the benefit of any parish or district is to be made, unless the Incumbent himself shall apply, or sanction the application for aid, and shall furnish to the Committee sufficient proof of the exigency of the case. The nomination of an Assistant shall always be left with the Clergyman to whom aid is given—the Committee claiming only full satisfaction as to the qualifications of his Nominee; who, when approved, will be under engagement only to the Clergyman by whom he is employed, and be solely responsible to him. Grants from the Society towards the support of an Assistant are made to the Clergyman to whom aid is given, and are voted for one year.

The names of the Officers of the Society who were appointed at its commencement:—

President.
His Grace the Duke of Manchester.

Vice-Presidents.
The Most Hon. the Marquis of Blandford, M.P.
The Right Hon. the Earl of Clancarty.
The Right Hon. the Earl of Roden.
The Right Hon. the Earl of Cavan.
The Right Hon. the Earl of Bandon.
The Right Hon. the Viscount Lifford.
The Right Hon. Lord Ashley, M.P.
The Right Hon. Viscount Bernard, M.P.
The Lord Henry Cholmondeley.
The Right Rev. the Lord Bishop of Cashel.
The Right Rev. the Lord Bishop of Tuam.
The Right Hon. Lord Dunsany.
Dr. Macbride, Principal of Magdalen Hall, Oxford.

Committee.

The Hon. Captain Maude.
The Hon. Arthur Kinnaird.
The Hon. Somerset Maxwell.
Sir T. W. Blomefield, Bart.
Sir Digby Mackworth, Bart.
Joseph Napier, Esq., M.P.
John P. Plumptre, Esq., M.P.
C. A. Moody, Esq., M.P.
Geo. A. Hamilton, Esq., M.P.
Sir W. Verner, Bart., M.P.
Charles H. Frewen, Esq., M.P.
Rear-Admiral Hope.
J. C. Colquhoun, Esq.
Anthony Lefroy, Esq.
Admiral Vernon Harcourt.
Rev. E. Hollond.
Rev. Daniel Wilson.
Rev. T. R. Birks.

Rev. W. Cadman.
Rev. M. M. Preston.
Rev. John Heming.
Rev. T. Nolan.
W. Garnier, Esq.
Captain Trotter.

John Dean Paul, Esq.
J. E. Gordon, Esq.
Alexander Gordon, Esq.
John Bridges, Esq.
Robert B. Seeley, Esq.
Evan Baillie, Esq.

Treasurer.
John Dean Paul, Esq., Messrs. Strahan, Paul, and Co.

Honorary Secretaries.
The Rev. Alexander R. C. Dallas, M.A., Wonston Rectory.
The Rev. Robert Bickersteth, M.A.

Clerical Secretary.—The Rev. William Wilkinson, B.A.
Assistant Secretary.—John Knott, Esq.
Office of the Society.—14, Exeter Hall, London.

THE PRESENT OFFICE BEARERS.
Vice-Presidents.
The Marquis of Cholmondeley. | The Earl of Shaftesbury.
The Earl of Roden, etc., etc.

Chairman of Committee.—J. C. Colquhoun, Esq.

Treasurers.
Hon. Arthur Kinnaird, M.P. | Capt. the Hon. F. Maude, R.N.

Council for Missions.
Rev. Alex. R. C. Dallas, *Chairman.*

Rev. E. Auriol.
Rev. T. R. Birks.

Rev. Ed. H. Bickersteth.
Lt.-Col. M. J. Rowlandson.

Rev. H. C. Cory, *Missionary Secretary.*

Hon. Sec. for Missions.—The Rev. Alex. R. C. Dallas, M.A.

Hon. Secretaries.
Rev. Sir C. Lighton, Bart., M.A. | Rev. J. B. Owen, M.A.

Secretary.—Lieutenant-Colonel F. S. Gabb.

London Bankers.—Ransom, Bouverie, & Co., Pall Mall East; Williams, Deacon, & Co., Birchin Lane.

Offices of the Society.—11, Buckingham Street, Adelphi, London, W.C.; and 12, D'Olier Street, Dublin.

Post Office Orders to be drawn on Charing Cross, payable to WILLIAM PASLEY, *Assistant Secretary.*

www.ingramcontent.com/pod-product-compliance
Lightning Source LLC
Chambersburg PA
CBHW031747230426
43669CB00007B/528